British history traditionally has been accorded a special place in the curricula of Canadian schools and universities. When universities were established in the last century, Canada was still regarded as part of the greater British nation and knowledge of British history was an essential prerequisite for good citizenship. Even before the establishment of formal history departments British historical studies existed as a separate subject.

In this book, Paul T. Phillips traces the position of British history in the universities and shows how Canada's changing relationship with Britain has affected the history curriculum. Canadian history began to develop as a distinct field in the early twentieth century, though it was often linked with British history, since the two subjects were frequently taught by the same person. The British background and training of many academics also ensured the continuing importance of British history at most universities until the 1950s.

The growth of nationalistic sentiment, ethnic changes in the population, and the loosening of Empire and Commonwealth ties contributed to diminished interest in British history in the 1960s and 1970s and saw the formal partitioning of British and Canadian history.

'Britain's Past in Canada' provides a unique perspective on Canada's evolving cultural identity. Many of the historians discussed—among them Sir Daniel Wilson, Goldwin Smith, Frank Underhill, Bertie Wilkinson, and A.R.M. Lower—were public figures deeply committed to various causes relating to national issues of the day. In addition, Canadian historians living abroad added to the intellectual life of Canada and the English-speaking world through their work. Phillips' examination of their neglected contribution brings new insights into the study of prominent Canadians outside Canada.

Paul T. Phillips is a professor and chairman of the Department of History at St. Francis Xavier University.

D1519146

BRITAIN'S PAST IN CANADA

The Teaching and Writing
of British History   Paul T. Phillips

UNIVERSITY OF BRITISH COLUMBIA PRESS
VANCOUVER 1989

ISBN 0-7748-0329-0 (cloth)
0-7748-0332-0 (paper)

Canadian Cataloguing in Publication Data

Phillips, Paul T., 1942-
Britain's past in Canada

Includes bibliographical references and index.
ISBN 0-7748-0329-0 (bound). — ISBN
0-7748-0332-0 (pbk.)

1. Great Britain – History – Study and
teaching (Higher) – Canada.   2. Great Britain –
Historiography.   I. Title.
DA4.P48 1989   941'.007'1171   C89-091276-9

This book has been published with the assistance of a grant
from the Canada Council.

Printed on acid-free paper

TO BARBARA

CONTENTS

PREFACE

The old British Empire is dead and many Canadians today seem un-concerned about their heritage. Yet we are still affected by our roots whether we like it or not. If we want to know more about ourselves, we must consider that through most of its existence Canada has been involved with Britain. This relationship has been both reflected in and influenced by the writing and teaching of history in this country.

The original aim of this book was to acquaint the reader with the current activities of one fairly specialized sector of Canadian university life. In time, the scope of the book changed, becoming more of a history of historians of Britain and of historians in general, and stretching beyond the confines of academe. This seemed a justifiable enlargement given the historian's urge to tell a story. The resulting product therefore has become something of a hybrid, being intended as much for a general readership as for professors, teachers, and students of history. For the sake of readability, notes have been limited, as have some conventions of the academic writing style. One of my objects also has been to depict some of the people presented here in very human terms, by recounting an anecdote or two that may be revealing or by allowing some latitude in an interview. But as the reader will see, there never was as much of a barrier between the life of the academic and the "outside world" as some would suppose.

If *Britain's Past in Canada* seems more a piece of popular history than a rigorous academic work, I shall not be upset. I would be more upset if readers thought that the stories of people discussed here were gossip for internal professional consumption. I believe that historians have always been concerned with their public, whether as teachers, as the writers of books, or in other capacities. In that sense their involvement with the wider society has counted for more than their relationships within academic departments. As this book will reveal, teachers of history have not only moulded young minds, but also between 1900 and about 1945 were seen as the prime dispensers of wisdom above and beyond the subject-matter. Since then other disciplines such as economics and sociology have been sources of "extra-scholarly wisdom," as a distinguished colleague has described the phenomenon, and today fewer people seem disturbed by George Santayana's observation that men who can't remember the past are condemned to repeat it.

The chapters that follow tell a story in more or less the old narrative way. In many places I have presented synthetic treatments, as there are available many excellent, more detailed historical studies about Canada for those who wish to explore its history in depth. In other places my archival and interview research has produced more specialized and original results. Though Chapter 1 covers 1900–45 in relation to its subject, Chapters 2–4 and 7 and 8 are chronologically ordered. Chapters 5 and 6 look at two important individuals, J. B. Brebner and Gerald Graham, whose careers peaked in the post-Second World War period. Brebner and Graham were also part of the Canadian community resident abroad who nonetheless made significant contributions to Canada's intellectual life.

Much of the material for the early chapters has been obtained from university archives in central Canada, not because central Canadians have been solely responsible for the development of the profession in this country, but because a number of their university departments, especially that of the University of Toronto, played an inordinately large role in the inception of the discipline in Canada. For better or worse, they established certain attitudes and patterns of behaviour that also developed elsewhere. As we would say in the Maritimes, "Upper Canadians" must be given credit where it is due. In focusing on British history and its early emphasis upon constitutional (and economic) developments, one also sees a link to the ideals of public service and patriotism that go well beyond the Ivory Tower, though many such attitudes had their roots among a relatively small group of academics teaching mainly at a relatively small number of schools in English Canada. On the other hand, the values inspired by history have never been simply products of university history departments.

BRITAIN'S PAST IN CANADA

CHAPTER ONE

CANADIANS AND THEIR HISTORY

It is difficult to discover when English-speaking Canadians ceased to think of themselves as British. The conventional dates marking the legislative autonomy of the Dominion in this century or the last are not a barometer of popular emotions on this issue. The process of Canadianization was a slow one over many generations and varied from place to place. As a boy in Toronto, I well remember the seriousness with which people treated events such as Elizabeth II's coronation. Symbols of the Empire such as Victoria Day or a Loyalist anniversary were ever-present. There were also symbols of the imperial connection, such as the equestrian statue of Edward VII in Queen's Park, moved in 1969 from India to Toronto by local subscription. Today few people have much special devotion to such memorabilia, but this is a very recent development. Areas like Montreal's Westmount may still reflect this sentiment.

Canada's transition from colonial status to independence was accomplished peacefully, with a great deal of positive feeling shown toward Britain. Part of why this is so may lie in the British genius for governing, Britain's leaders having learned valuable lessons from the American Revolution. The Commonwealth idea of a looser confederacy of culturally linked autonomous states as in ancient Greece perhaps was a vague concept informing British policy decisions long before this century. There is also the possibility in the case of Upper Canada at least, as suggested by Fred Schneider, that collaboration (not in the pejorative sense) based upon a habit of deference toward Britain's governing class was responsible for much of the orderly transfer of power.[1] Certainly Canadians have prided themselves on their sense of law and order and disciplined conduct in contrast to their neighbours south of the border. In this respect the British inheritance has often been linked to such attitudes.

It was therefore only natural in past generations that English-speaking adult Canadians would assume that children should be reared revering the British connection, as they themselves were. Such indoctrination was effected principally through the study of history. Thus much of the school history taught in the nineteenth and early twentieth centuries in Canada was British. As the distinguished Canadian historian, Arthur Lower, said of his early youth: "I don't think anybody ever suspected that there was any other kind of history. And we had history in the public school, we had history in the high school, and we had history in Varsity, and it was all English history."[2] The earliest history school texts were, of course, bland compendia of facts for memorization. Egerton Ryerson, chief superintendent of schools from 1844 to 1876, apparently viewed some of the earlier American influences on Upper Canadian schools as insidious because he believed that anti-British texts were used in areas supportive of the 1837 rebellion.[3]

After 1850 the Council of Public Instruction therefore produced an authorized list of textbooks for the province. In time other provinces were influenced by the Ryerson model and opted for prescribed single texts in various subject areas, establishing what some observers might feel is a Canadian obsession for bland uniformity.

Evident in this system of social discipline was the care with which texts were written and approved. Many history texts were reprints of British editions but nonetheless were thought appropriate for Canada.[4] Nova Scotia, for example, very early used a text entitled *Outlines of the History of England for Families and Schools* published in London in 1845 and distributed by the Society for the Propagation of Christian Knowledge. Ryerson about the same time was introducing revised texts in Upper Canada originally used as "Irish National Readers." By the 1860s A.W. MacKinlay had begun to co-publish the Nelson's School series in Halifax, which included William Francis Collier's *History of the British Empire*, an 1868 text which revealed some early concern with social history. Political history, however, was the standard basis of presentation. The parliamentary form of government was thought to be Britain's major contribution to world civilization. Commonly connected with this political emphasis was the strong acceptance of the Whig-Liberal interpretation of history. The ideas of William Stubbs and other Liberal historians had a dominant influence over textbook presentations. Today many professional historians have reappraised such historical views because of their simplistic view of English history as the struggle for liberty against reactionary kings, royalists, and Roman Catholics.

Frank Underhill once reflected on the effect of these ideas on him as a schoolboy:

> The teaching we got in our schools and in our universities
> was mostly on the left as concerns England, that is the
> Puritans were right against the Cavaliers, and the Whigs
> were right against the Tories, the radicals were right
> against the reactionaries of the late 19th century. At high
> school I was brought up on Green's [J.R. Green] *History of
> the English People*. Well, that was good left-wing Liberal
> history. I thought that was a straight statement of facts and
> it was only when I became more mature, that I realized that
> it was a very one-sided statement of the Liberal point of
> view of English history.[5]

Noting history teaching's one-sidedness did not prevent Underhill
and other historians from articulating ideological positions later in
life not so different from those of their Whig mentors. James T.
Shotwell also reflected on the same school text in another context:
"Green was a nationalist. He began over in Germany and paid no
attention to the Britons. If ever there was a mixed people it is the
English but Green paid no attention to the mixture. He had a nineteenth century view and paralleled German historians of the same
period, fortunately not with the same theme of achievement as the
Germans and especially the Prussians."[6]

Again one can only imagine the effect of the racial admiration
for Teutons evident in the writing of Edward Augustus Freeman
and other Liberal writers of the same school. In spite of Shotwell's
reservations, he admired Green's prose, especially his description
of seventeenth-century figures. As Shotwell put it, "If you have a
master of the art of history he can leave you something even if
the content has to be revised later."[7] Whig history, of course, was
not confined to English writers. W. J. Robertson, Principal of St.

Catharines Collegiate Institute in Ontario, for example, wrote a *Public School History of England and Canada* published by Copp Clark in 1897. Many traces of the same attitudes extended even to the "wise and merciful tyranny" of Cromwell.[8] Virtually all nineteenth- and early twentieth-century textbooks praised the overall accomplishments of Britain, especially its "genius" for government. As Robertson stated: "After nineteen centuries of strife and struggle, England stands in the forefront of nations, fresh and vigorous, every pulse throbbing with a healthy national life, her 'eyes not dim and her natural strength not abated'."[9]

In this context some complaints were made about the *English* bias in the teaching of British history. In an 1866 letter to the Chief Superintendent of Education on the merits of White's *History of Great Britain and Ireland,* Spencer Jones, the Master of a rural Canada West (Ontario) grammar school stated: "I prefer White's History, chiefly because it is the only one of its size and cost that I am acquainted with, that contains a detailed account of the history of *each* of the three kingdoms. This renders it a special favorite with parents of children of Scottish and Irish origin who from other works only learn incidentally something about that part of the empire in which they are more immediately interested."[10]

Forty years later Mary Leslie urged that the Ontario Ministry of Education adopt her *Historic Sketches of Scotland,* arguing that:

> There is no separate history of Scotland taught in the Public Schools. It is merely a skeleton outline merged in the study of Great Britain. Scotland has not only a political history of its own, but a literature of its own, traditional records, songs, ballads, and folklore, and at least, one third of the population of Canada is of Scottish descent, I think

some distinct account of the country and people deserve a
place in the Public Schools.[11]

As Arthur Lower was to observe of his upbringing, rightly or
wrongly there was "not even any reference to Scotland" in the all-
English history taught in public and high schools.[12]

Any wavering in the required emphasis on British achievements
usually brought down wrath on a perpetrator. Small wonder, then,
that a public outcry arose in 1893 when the Liberal government of
Ontario proposed to omit questions in British history from the high
school entrance examination. The Honourable G.W. Ross, Minister of Education, quickly replied to criticism in the Legislature.
"It's a mistake to think," he said, "that the Ontario Government
does not sympathize with the British connection. Every man Jack
of us is in favour of it."[13] He also answered Opposition critics by
arguing that under the present system there was actually more
danger of a teacher inculcating "annexation sentiment" through a
distortion of British history.

Undercurrents concerning the teaching of British history ran
deep. One opposition member tied changes in the examination requirements to modifications in the existing textbook: "'Bloody
Mary,' for instance, has been omitted no doubt in deference to a
certain vote; and in another place Protestantism is spoken of as
'the new religion'—a grievous error, seeing that Protestantism is as
old as Christ."[14] Provost Charles W. Body of Trinity College, W.J.
Robertson, and others when deliberating the use of authorized
textbooks for the schools had had similar quibbles about passages
that impinged on Protestantism. It was clear that the proper teaching of British history was held by some to be closely allied to
Ontario's Protestant hegemony. The Toronto *Empire* argued con-

cerning the reinstatement of British history as a requirement for high school admission: "The rising generation shall go out into the world with some pride in their forefathers, with some knowledge of the race which has fought for civil and religious liberty, and with some appreciation of the grand principles and achievements taught in British history."[15] Many parents were themselves British immigrants and wanted to ensure that their children were fully aware of their heritage.

A similar outcry occurred in British Columbia on at least two occasions. One concerned the banning in 1920 of a textbook on Canadian history by W.L. Grant for allegedly containing anti-British sentiments.[16] Two years later Mack Eastman, the first professor of history at the University of British Columbia, was castigated by one Canon Hinchcliffe in the provincial legislature for choosing anti-British books for student use. Eastman resolutely defended the choice of American written texts, arguing in one case that the frontispiece showed "British troops victorious," which "has excited the wrath of the enemies of Britain in the United States."[17] However, despite Eastman's disclaimers, suspicion of American texts remained and the final contracts for textbooks normally went to British or Canadian authors and publishers.

Outside the public school system there were, of course, other sorts of schools which inculcated the virtues of the British way of life. Jean Barman has described the importation of the British public school ideal in British Columbia in *Growing Up British in British Columbia* (1984). Similar schools could be found in central Canada and the Maritimes. Colonial mentalities clearly persisted at many of these institutions well into the twentieth century. As Goldwin Smith wrote in 1895 to the Ontario Minister of Education on the appointment of a new headmaster for Upper Canada Col-

lege: "I wish, if Nativist principle does not forbid, you may get a
man from one of the great English public schools. Those men are
experts in the management of a *particular class* of boys, and we
have no means of producing them here."[18] It is ironic that
W.L. Grant, author of the heretical "anti-British" Canadian history text mentioned earlier, was once headmaster of this very
school.

The demand for Canadian history increased after 1900. Frequently it could be found as a small supplement to British history
texts. The early authors of texts devoted to Canada such as Sir
C.P. Lucas and Sir Charles G.D. Roberts tended to be as enthusiastic supporters of the British as any Briton writing British history.
G.U. Hay noted at the beginning of his *Public School History of
Canada* (1901): "Where are the boys and girls who are not proud
of such a land, who are not eager to help make it their home, and
to preserve it as a part of our great British Empire!" It may be
argued that many an early history of Canada was not the history of
Canada as Canada at all. As the Toronto *Globe* noted in defence of
having Canadian history questions in place of British during the
Ontario examination crisis of 1893, "is not every object of Canadian history from the conquest of Canada in 1759 down to the present time, a reflex of British history?"[19] As late as 1939 the *Nova
Scotia Journal of Education* noted of history at the Grade 10 level:
"It is suggested that pupils should not begin the study of Canada
until English History to the end of the chapter entitled 'The Industrial Revolution' has been taught. During the study of Canadian
History frequent reference should be made to contemporary events
in English and world history" (p 424).

Long before 1939 dissatisfaction was registered with how history
was taught. For example, Kenneth Bell, a lecturer in the Univer-

sity of Toronto history department and an Englishman, in 1910 wrote thus about history teaching in the schools: "So much for four things which history is not. It is not an expanded form of 'Rule Britannia.' It is not a suitable trapeze for mental gymnastics. It is not a subject to be got up as a passport to citizenship; and it is not a series of *formulae* to be acquired as a mental outfit for all the emergencies of a would-be teacher—a teacher's *Vade mecum.*"[20]

Many introspective debates ensued in the years that followed concerning the nature of history in the schools. In 1919, for example, a committee of university and high school history teachers wrote to John Seath, Ontario Superintendent of Education, urging that high school history courses be broadened beyond British and Canadian studies to include ancient and continental history. There was also the disturbing news that a questionnaire circulated to entrance students in education in 1917 indicated that poetry far outdistanced history as a source of reading for pleasure. In the interests of ending both the "narrowness" and the "endless repetition" of the existing program, a new curriculum was recommended.

Some ten years later Walter Sage of the University of British Columbia history department made one of the most comprehensive reports on history teaching in elementary schools. The report covered the entire country, noting the content and purpose of history teaching in the various provinces. Sage observed that there was no national uniformity in teaching objectives. Quebec was quite separate, instilling its own regional pride but with little reference to larger considerations, including the British connection. In English-speaking Quebec Catholic schools there was provision for the teaching of Irish history only. Though Ontario was "noted for its loyalty to the British Empire," shown in its emphasis on British and Canadian history, it was Manitoba and British Columbia that provided the most comprehensive approach (as opposed to divisions into many periods) to Britain's past.[21] In this respect perhaps the two western provinces foresaw the danger of chopping British history into sections, thereby continuing the study of "great themes" in the sweep of centuries.

The insularity of Quebec's French-speaking schools was of long standing. While usually loyal to the symbols of British authority, suspicion of "Anglo" values in religious and secular thought was nonetheless present. The praise for Lord Durham's report (including his prophesy of the demise of the French language) by respected figures such as Sir Charles "God Damn" Roberts could not help but reconfirm French Quebecers' suspicions of English textbooks. In any case, few English historians' writings were available in French at this time.

The issue of objectives in history teaching had been taken up with greater directness by members of the University of Toronto history department in 1923 when it warned against the use of history as propaganda. At the same time the proposal to publish "golden books" revealing the noble British spirit for primary and secondary students appears to have been no departure from past tradition.[22] Indeed, the British and Canadian history texts produced by G.M. Wrong, head of the U of T history department in this period, clearly exemplified the Whig-Liberal tradition and devotion to Empire.

The interwar period saw Canada gain virtually full sovereignty within the newly defined Empire-Commonwealth. It also witnessed a growing continentalist attitude on the part of intellectuals such as Frank Underhill, but school texts were slow to reflect the new attitudes. Even during the Second World War, unfavourable comparisons were made between the glorious evolution of the Commonwealth and the American Revolution—"the Declaration of Equality" versus "the Declaration of Independence" as one textbook put it.[23] The study of American history and Canadian-American relations received less attention, apart from emphasis upon the sin of the American Revolution. The American Council on Education produced a report which commented upon this situation in 1947:

> In general, authors of textbooks in British history give a fair, though inadequate treatment of Canadian-American relations. However, there are some exceptions to this in some textbooks where there are instances of a pro-British point of view. For example, in the treatment of the causes of the American Revolution most of these Canadian texts in British history present a one-sided picture of the background and immediate causes of the war. Little attempt is made to explain the colonial point of view. [24]

From the Canadian point of view the report failed to distinguish between how a Canadian attitude on the American Revolution might differ from a pro-British one. The difference never has been defined. As late as the 1960s, perhaps in deference to the Loyalist tradition, the American version of the Revolution was handled with care in the Canadian national media. By then, however, many had accepted the view that the colonists had been mistreated but that the revolution was not inevitable.[25]

Textbooks by older historians such as George Wrong were still in circulation in the late 1940s, though a new attitude was slowly working its way into such materials in the post-Second World War era. By the 1950s it had become necessary to explain *why* Canadian students should study British history. As Richard Lambert, supervisor for CBC school broadcasts, wrote in *The Great Heritage* (1958): "Our system of popular responsible government, our tradition of individual freedom, our incorruptible law courts, the useful and often beautiful English language, the bonds of Commonwealth and our beloved monarchy—all these heritages were founded in Britain. To protect them, we must understand them" (p v).

The mandatory explanation for studying British history in Canadian schools coincided with its relegation to a subordinate position in the curriculum. In time, with the possible exception of New Brunswick, it became an optional subject of instruction. It is quite true that Canadian history courses contained a healthy dose of British history, but it was no longer a special subject in most provinces. In Newfoundland there was also some delay in subordinating British history, the province having been a British colony until 1949. The valuable observation made in some 1950s school texts about the cultural unity of the English-speaking peoples was not developed. On the wider stage of world politics, the replacement of Britain by the United States as our "protector" was not translated into the history syllabus. Detailed knowledge of American history was not proportionately advanced. This may have been a reaction to the suggestion that Canada was becoming a "client" state of the Americans. It may also have been a holdover of the generations-old attitude, going back to Ryerson, that Canadians must curb insidious Americanizing influences in schools. The admonition to "know thy enemy" apparently was never seriously considered.

It is not for the historian or journalist to lament such developments. It is simply part of the natural evolution in a society's attitudes. But one *can* say that the awareness of the world in general, and of our heritage in particular, has been diminished by dropping British history in the schools. Granted that for most of the imperial "heyday" teaching British history in school was largely indoctrination. It was also highly English-centred, as Lower observed. Repeated pleas to broaden the syllabus to include more about the Scots and Irish had gone largely unheeded since Victorian times. School children nevertheless gleaned much useful information in the process. Later in their lives their knowledge of British history undoubtedly made Canadian customs, law, government, and even language more intelligible. In that sense a framework that had brought some cultural cohesion at least to English Canada has been lost since 1945.

Lost also has been popular history reading which unified the Empire, which ranged from the scholarly works of Lord Macaulay and J.R. Seeley to the historical fiction of Sir Walter Scott and G.A. Henty. This substratum of beliefs, nurtured in dignified as well as vulgar ways, probably made most English Canadians agree with the arguments of Sir Charles Lucas in *The British Empire* (1920). In Lucas's view, the Empire had been created to sustain and advance political and religious liberty as much as for economic gain. Its positive and expanding mission, he believed, had benefitted English and non-English peoples alike. Noting that some forms of nationalism bred in this tolerant policy of diversity showed signs of discontent, Lucas pointed out that French Canadians or Dutch Boers would at the same time "refuse to exchange their present position for a place in any other empire or group of communities" (p 221). With the ending of all European empires except the Soviet, such considerations became merely nostalgia.

Massive immigration from non-English speaking countries since the Second World War has also changed Canadians' perception of the nation. Ethnic considerations must have expression in schools. However, knowledge of British history might also have helped Italians or Slovaks to understand how certain institutions and customs had evolved in their new homeland. By the time those immigrants arrived, the racist and Whiggish bias of the old histories was already waning, if not dead. Elliot Rose of the University of Toronto has noted the rather strict direction against prejudicial views given by Copp Clark to authors for the preparation of *The Modern Era* in 1960.[26] But this is now the tale of what might have been. It is ironic that Canada and Canadians abroad in the 1970s and 1980s have produced an unprecedented crop of excellent textbooks in British history—namely those by Michael Powicke, J.R. Lander, Wayne State's Goldwin Smith, J.B. Conacher, T.O. Lloyd, Robert Malcolmson, Albert Tucker, and one or two others. For these writers the wider themes and scope of British history have not been forgotten.

For many Canadians before the 1960s, a visit to Britain was not altogether an excursion to a foreign land. A cultural Commonwealth existed which for most people included at least common knowledge of certain fundamental facts whether one was born in Saskatchewan or Sussex. Canadians, though separated by a common language from their British cousins, as in Bernard Shaw's view of Americans, did not then require interpreters of cultural differences. Today we are in as much need of an Alastair Cooke as are residents of the republic to the south.

CHAPTER TWO

BIRTH
OF A
DISCIPLINE

British history was an essential part of the curricula of early Canadian universities, and even predated the founding of most university history departments, reflecting not only the sense of allegiance to Britain but also necessity. University faculties were so small in the last century that a number of subjects frequently had to be taught by one professor. There was another and more profound reason, however. History as a distinct discipline only gained recognition in the late nineteenth century. Surprisingly, the idea that history was a subject that could stand on its own was quite new when compared to the established disciplines such as literature, philosophy, and mathematics.

Academics and others had written history books for some time, but as a separate discipline, requiring specific training for its practitioners and professional standards for judging excellence, history was in its infancy in the last century. Professionals in related areas such as law or political philosophy were apt to see his-

tory merely as a tool to be used as they saw fit. Much changed in
the Victorian age. For one thing, more of the general public developed a historical consciousness, partly as a result of increased lit-
eracy and partly because of more widespread higher education.

The popularity of history books was greatly influenced by the
historical novels of such writers as Sir Walter Scott. Scott in particular had a remarkable impact upon his readership. Despite his
tendency to handle historical settings romantically, he inspired interest in times past. He was a good social historian because of his
ability to capture the atmosphere of bygone days, without being a
social historian by training or a meticulous dispenser of historical
facts.

One who did revere facts but nonetheless had been inspired
by Scott was Leopold Von Ranke. This most renowned of all nineteenth-century historians, in reacting against the tendency of earlier Enlightenment writers to ridicule or polemicize aspects of the
past, believed that writers of history should approach their subjects with reverence, sympathy, and above all, understanding. He
became the champion of the archives, urging his own seminar students in Germany and ultimately those in other countries to search
out facts in order to discover historical events "as they really
were." In arguing that students of history learn how their predeces-
sors thought in order to explain their actions, Ranke helped create
a trend in German historical circles which came to be known as
"historicism."

Though Ranke adopted an empirical approach based on thorough research in archives, it was the disciples of the French philosopher Auguste Comte and the English writer Henry Thomas
Buckle who advanced the idea that history should be seen as a
science. Rejecting the study of the peculiarities of individual past

events and historical accident, the scientific historians switched from focusing upon the particular to focusing upon the general. Believing that observed similarities and common patterns in history could lead to the discovery of *laws* similar to those employed by natural scientists, the Postivists, as they were called, acquired a number of adherents. One of the most famous was J.B. Bury, who upon gaining the Regius professorship at Oxford in 1902, declared history to be a science "no more and no less."

Eventually some historians became sceptical of such a claim and created a rival group known as the Idealists. They argued that the discipline of history demanded particular methodological approaches. For some time, however, the idea of history as a science captured the imagination of Victorian scholars. Then in the midst of this debate, through the publication in Germany of *The Life of Jesus* by David Friedrich Strauss in 1835, the controversies were fuelled by the application of the historian's archival research to sacred scripture. Would the Bible stand up to the historian's scrutiny? Such investigations unsettled scholars and public alike.

Notwithstanding these disturbing thoughts, historical works could also be enjoyed by the general public. Macaulay's books on English history sold enormously well; in fact, no one rivalled him in this regard until Arnold Toynbee in our own times. Macaulay became the first historian to be given a peerage. A wonderful writer, he preached the concept of intellectual and moral improvement as seen through the unfolding of politics. His Whig-Liberal bias and literary style spawned a host of imitators and nurtured many generations of young minds in the values he professed. George Bancroft, who mixed nationalism with the doctrine of progress, not unlike Macaulay, had similar though not equal success in the United States. Such splendid writers made many people realize that history touched the lives of all men. But such persuasive writers were also somewhat at odds with the intentions at least of more research-oriented younger scholars, who argued that newer, more professional approaches should be applied to the study of history.[1]

At the ancient universities of the Empire, history was not taught as a separate discipline until the Victorian age, and certainly not by academics, who for the most part considered themselves professionals. Throughout much of the nineteenth century, classics were considered to be the core of a university curriculum. At Oxford, for example, a School of Law and modern History was established at mid-century, but history was to be studied only after taking the "Litterae Humaniores" or "Greats" curriculum. Although most students by then aspired to careers in the civil service rather than in the church, classics was still seen as the fount of wisdom for life as well as livelihood.

General educated opinion, however, favoured advance of the discipline. The Public Record Office and the Historical Manuscripts Commission came into existence about this time, providing more new materials for original research. The university reforms of the 1850s and 1860s also helped the historian, as did the shift to full-time "scientific" professionals from men of letters in most university faculties, as described by T. W. Heyck.[2] The literate public also supported the election of bona fide scholars to various history professorships created in the eighteenth and nineteenth centuries. Prior to the mid-nineteenth century, professors did not need to be research-oriented or even scholars. Late nineteenth-century Oxford and Cambridge saw a succession of illustrious names attached to the various professorships of history. As Philippa Levine has indicated, research degrees developed very slowly, with the Oxford B.Litt., for example, appearing only in 1895 and the D.Phil. in 1917.[3] Even such influential exponents of training in Rankean methods as William Stubbs had a limited impact upon students before 1914.

The Oxford Honours School of Modern History, which emerged in the 1870s and gained the lion's share of undergraduate enrolments in the next generation, was controlled by tutors, not by research professors. As Reba Sofer has shown, tutors resisted professionalization of training, believing that reading history was more a vehicle for inspiring correct values than for creation of future scholars.[4] This may have retarded the development of some potential professional practitioners, but given the large number of students, it may well have helped to put history in the forefront of school curricula by the outbreak of the First World War. Within the highest ranks of academe, however, "research and specialized study by a secular as well as a professional body of scholars and scientists dominated the scene" by 1900.[5]

Colonial universities followed roughly the same pattern as those in Britain. History was taught in mid-Victorian times but usually subsumed under another subject. Classics was the central subject and while not always commanding the disciples of Clio, did cast its shadow over many who wished to study the past. Greek and Roman history consumed the attention of many students, "modern" history being of less interest. However, Freeman, Stubbs, and others made early modern history respectable and university calendars and examination papers reveal that the history of seventeenth-century England was being taught by the 1880s.

At Dalhousie University a chair of rhetoric and history was established as early as 1865 within a total faculty complement of five for arts and sciences. Of necessity, interdisciplinary approaches had to be used, history being coupled with classics, rhetoric, or, increasingly, English literature. In the Stubbs tradition, constitutional history was usually stressed and benefited from the fact that it could be taught by lawyers. British history lectures, for example, were given by Richard Weldon, an eminent professor of international law, as well as by Jacobi De Mill until 1880 and after that by the Reverend John Forrest, the first George Munro Professor of History and Political Economy.

At the University of Toronto Sir Daniel Wilson was appointed professor of history and English literature in 1853. Though Wilson's career was to be associated mainly with university administration and research in ethnology, he regularly taught courses in English history. His qualifications to teach history were quite good for that time. A friend of both the English historians Henry Hallam and Robert Vaughan, he had written and published a book on Oliver Cromwell and the Protectorate in 1848.[6] His book had been well received by a number of learned British journals, though it was not a work of original research. Wilson betrayed a clear love for Cromwell much like Carlyle, who had recently attempted to rehabilitate the seventeenth-century Puritan leader. As Wilson stated in the preface: "His virtues are mostly so far above those of the great majority of England's hereditary kings, that the injustice, which excludes the greatest of all her rulers from that vacant niche between the two Charles Stuarts, is a wrong done far more to us than to him." Wilson's admiration of Cromwell's adherence to truth and liberty extended even to the latter's infamous Irish campaign, in which his suppression of the Catholics was justified on the grounds of earlier attacks by papists on Protestants, which "scarcely paralleled in the tortures of the red Indian, or the hideous feasts of South Sea savages" (p 144).

In his years at the University of Toronto, Wilson's true interests lay not in history but in his personal crusade against Darwin's theory of evolution through his numerous anthropological studies and his continuing love of English literature. It was therefore somewhat of a blow to him when, in 1888, the chairs of English literature and history were separated and he was made the first professor of history.

His "bad luck" was further compounded by the great fire of 1890 in University College, where thousands of books were destroyed as well as Wilson's personal papers. As he noted in his diary on 9 March 1891:

> Have fagged to-day at two lectures, one for my 2nd year on the reign of Edward III, the era of Chaucer and William of Wykeham, and also of the Black Prince and Cressy and Poitiers; the other for my third year's was on the War of Spanish Succession, and the brilliant Augustan age of that poor royal mediocrity, Queen Anne—a charming subject —both indeed charming themes, if one had time. But the burning of my whole 37 years of accumulated lecture notes has been very hard on me. Started afresh; and each day is a scramble, in spite of a tolerably well-stored memory. I think of poor old Hincks whom we used to laugh at most unsympathetically as he moaned over the loss of a box of old sermons that went down in the "Annie-Jane." But the old spirit is wanting with which I used to sketch out a new lecture, and look to polishing and giving it poignancy in future years. I cannot hope for such now.[7]

Wilson was assisted in the teaching of history in his tenure as professor by William J. Ashley, later knighted, who arrived from Lincoln College, Oxford, in 1888. Though an economic historian,
Ashley was appointed professor of constitutional history, a position
independent of both Wilson and his teaching associates in Greek
and Roman history. Ashley lectured mainly in economic history,
and taught *some* English constitutional history to political science
and law students. Much of the practical work of teaching constitutional history was actually done by an assistant, J.M. McEvoy.[8]

Though born of Nonconformist parents in Bermondsey (his father was a journeyman hatter), Ashley had steadily moved into the
centre of national life, winning a history scholarship to Balliol College, Oxford, in 1878. As well as having graduated in the first
class of the honour school of modern history, his interests also embraced economics. Back at Oxford, the famous *Industrial Revolution,* not actually written by Arnold Toynbee but identified as his
work, was said to have been put together from the lecture notes of
William Ashley, among others. As well, the Oxford Economic Society first met in Ashley's rooms at Lincoln College a year before
his departure to Canada. Ashley by then was a university lecturer.

A powerful influence on him was the German "historical school"
of economics. Some German economists of the mid-nineteenth
century rejected earlier classical theories of laissez-faire, believing that economic systems were best understood in terms of
specific historical conditions rather than unchanging "laws."
Ashley was so impressed by Gustav Schmöller and other exponents
of the historical school that he became the leading spokesman of
this approach in England, simultaneously endorsing the idea of an
expanded role for the state. This approach clearly represented a
departure from the "Manchester school" of economic individu-

alism in which he had been nurtured. Ashley also began a slow migration toward Anglicanism that was fully completed some years later when he was in the United States. While at Oxford he had been a member of the National Church Reform Union, along with T.H. Green, and the Christian Social Union (CSU). The CSU was not only famous for its espousal of Christian socialism but also for the publication, through its Oxford branch, of *The Economic Review*.[9]

Even before going to Toronto in 1888, Ashley had had North American associations through these Oxford organizations. Principal J.P. Sheraton of Wycliffe College, for example, was a strong advocate of a rehabilitated national church, in keeping with the National Church Reform Union, and a CSU group had been formed on the University of Toronto campus. The university also operated a university settlement in the slum areas of the city modelled on the activities of British undergraduates inspired by Samuel Barnett and T.H. Green.

Shortly after taking up his appointment at Toronto, Ashley's *Introduction to English Economic History* was published. It revealed his strong advocacy of the German historical school, which was later reflected in his inaugural lecture at Toronto.[10] A kindred spirit could be found in Adam Shortt of Queen's University, who shared many of Ashley's Germanic ideas about educating the literate public and using economic history as a way of training university students in responsible statecraft.[11] His ideas about how to make history more into a science like geology were also in line with the social evolutionary notions of Auguste Comte.[12]

Ashley did not remain long at Toronto. Although he dabbled in some Canadian topics, much of his interest shifted to the United States, encouraged no doubt by his friend Richard T. Ely of Johns

Hopkins University. Ely shared a remarkable number of traits with Ashley, including conversion to Anglicanism (Episcopalianism in the United States) as well as devotion to the German historical school (unlike Ashley he had been educated in Germany).[13] When a position opened up at Harvard in 1892 it was too much for Ashley to resist. He emphasized in his resignation letter that he liked Toronto, but that the Harvard appointment was "a position in which I can devote myself almost entirely to the sort of work in which I am most interested, viz economic history."[14] Harvard had created the first chair of economic history in the English-speaking world especially for him, and Ashley soon began to have a major impact on American academe through his assaults upon the entrenched orthodoxy of laissez-faire economics. At Toronto he had left an important legacy by establishing interest in economic history that rivalled many important Canadian historians' interest in constitutional history in the early part of this century.

Many scholars lamented Ashley's departure from U of T, including Sir Daniel Wilson. Wilson's career in fact ended the year of Ashley's departure. Ashley had been a splendid colleague, but it is questionable whether he had been happy at Toronto, having been frustrated by low pay and an inability to move instruction in constitutional history into the history department. The latter situation was due mainly to the menacing influence (from the historians' viewpoint) of James Mavor of the political economy department.

The U of T, of course, was not devoid of other inspiring English academics at this time. One singularly important resident was Goldwin Smith. Smith easily could have been the nucleus of a modern history school at the university, having been both Regius

Professor of Modern History at Oxford and Professor of English History at Cornell.

He had, with the appropriate Liberal party connections, been appointed at the age of thirty-six to the Regius professorship, succeeding the less famous Halford Vaughan.[15] While at Oxford he had had much to do with reorganization at the ancient university, including ending Anglican exclusivity. Through his university and political involvement he had considerable dealings with the Liberal leader, William Gladstone, and thus incurred, on the other side, the wrath of Benjamin Disraeli. Smith later believed he was used by Disraeli as a living model for a derogatory character in *Lothair*. Disraeli's dislike of Smith, however, was as much for his anti-semitism as for his Liberal politics.

Smith's philosophy of history was in marked contrast to Ashley's. He disliked any form of determinism whether Darwinian or Comptean and hence was sceptical about ever making history a science. Though equally rejecting any sort of divine plan in history, Smith thought the "key" to the theory of history was in the "formation of man's character, which is pre-eminently religious and moral. . . . "[16] As he stated in his inaugural lecture of 1859: "I submitted that history is made up of the actions of men, and that each of us is conscious in his own case that the actions of men are free."[17]

Smith, like so many Victorian Liberals, also believed in the doctrine of inevitable progress. Such a faith, as far as he was concerned, required no explanation: "The progress of the human race is a truth of which everyday language is full; one which needs no logical proof and no rhetorical enforcement."[18]

Smith remained Regius Professor at Oxford only until 1868. He had interesting experiences in the years of his tenure, including instructing both the Prince of Wales and Prince Leopold of Belgium. As Malcolm Ross has pointed out, the consuming passion of Smith's life was journalism rather than straight history. His interest in the events and aftermath of the American Civil War had a profound effect upon him and led him to take up permanent residence in the "Great Democracy." No longer orthodox in his religious convictions, he once confided that his departure from England made it easier to withdraw from the Established Church. His father's death in 1868 brought an inheritance that in turn ended his Oriel fellowship. He was also facilitated in his decision to reside in North America by an invitation to join the faculty of the newly founded Cornell University.

At Cornell, Smith was professor of English history only until 1871, though he remained an emeritus professor thereafter and made many trips back to Ithaca. It is said that one of his reasons for leaving Cornell was the university decision to admit women as students. But his move to Toronto in 1871 was also motivated by the need to have a better base for his journalism as well as to be united with relatives. Soon he married into Canadian wealth, took up residence at his great house, "The Grange" (now part of the Art Gallery of Ontario), and became a major figure in Canadian public affairs until his death in 1910.

While much of Smith's time was taken up addressing topical issues of his day, founding and editing journals, and travelling, he remained interested in the historical profession and universities. Britain also continued to engage his mind, in particular its political history. As he once stated when describing England to Canadians: "Westminster is the centre of politics. It may be said historically to be the centre of politics, not for London and Great Britain only, but for the civilized world."[19]

Paradoxically, Goldwin Smith believed that Canada's future lay in increased co-operation with the United States. In this public posture he earned the disapproval of many English Canadians, which once cost him an honorary degree from the University of Toronto. However, whatever his anti-imperial view of the present situation in North America, he was quick to point out the value of British history:

> As an old country, England perhaps is naturally regarded first from the historical point of view, and especially by us of whose history she is the scene, whose monuments and the graves of whose ancestors she holds in her keeping. It is an advantage which Canadians have over Americans that they have not broken with their history and cast off the influences, at once exalting and sobering, which the record of a long and grand foretime exerts upon the mind of a community.[20]

As an éminence grise in academic circles Smith was deeply involved with the academic reorganization of the University of Toronto in 1906, even advising its administrators not to follow the path of athletics pursued by Oxford. As a historian he continued to have things to say about the profession and in turn was showered with honorary degrees and the presidency of the American Historical Association.

In his later years Smith had considerable contact with the young man who would succeed Wilson in the chair of history, George M.

Wrong. Wrong read and corrected the manuscript of Smith's *The United Kingdom: A Political History* (1899), a two-volume survey from the Norman conquest to the era of parliamentary reform. It also appears that Wrong was repaid a loan from sales of the book.[21] The history itself revealed Smith's staunch Liberalism, as he praised individuals and groups who advanced the various personal freedoms and rights of English subjects and damned monarchs such as James II ("he fancied himself the viceregent of God," p 55) who stood in the way. As he stated concerning Britain in general, "Islands seem dedicated by nature to freedom" (p 2).

By this time Smith also had developed a somewhat cynical view of the role of religion, or what masqueraded as religion in historical developments. He was consistently harsh in his comments about Roman Catholicism. In his Oxford inaugural lecture he confidently predicted the downfall of the papacy, which he regarded as "the grand cause of division in Christendom."[22] Yet in *The United Kingdom* he was equally harsh on Henry VIII for dissolution of the monasteries: "Rapine was not statesmanship, nor did it walk in statesmanlike ways" (p 335). In describing the lack of Protestant opposition to Bloody Mary, he noted that "probably not a single holder of abbey lands died for a cause to which he owed them" (p 364). Usually, like Wilson, he praised Cromwell, going back to his appraisal in the Oxford inaugural lecture when he described the Lord Protector as "the greatest statesman, perhaps, that the world ever saw," who "drew from Christianity, though tainted with Judaism, every principle, every idea, every expression of his public life" (p 151). Smith even attempted a mild defence of the infamous 1649 massacre of Drogheda in a work entitled *Irish History and the Irish Question* (1905). The book generally contained many criticisms of English policy and so received

praise from such Irishmen as Justin McCarthy and Horace
Plunkett. Smith was never one to avoid controversy.

Wilson, Smith, and Ashley were not only important figures in
Canadian academic life in their own time but also influenced the
man who was to expand the initial foundations of the historical discipline at the university level in Canada. Though lacking the professional credentials of his illustrious mentors, George Wrong was
to do much in a very practical way to make the profession viable in
this country.

CHAPTER THREE

THE RISING PROFESSION

It is perhaps not encouraging that the University of Toronto's first professor of history, Daniel Wilson, should have preferred the first chair of English literature and that McGill's, Charles Colby, eventually quit to manage a typewriter business. However, the profession was in luck with the appointment of George Wrong as second professor of history in Canada's largest university.

Wrong's career did not begin in the best of circumstances. The young historian was not in fact formally trained in history at all. Though he fell under the sway of Goldwin Smith and befriended William Ashley, he was by training a moral philosopher and student of divinity.

Born into an old Loyalist family in Port Burwell, Canada West (Ontario), in 1860, George was reared in impoverished gentility. His father lost the family farm four years after George was born and became a tradesman in nearby Vienna. George was fortunate in being able to study in the good local grammar school and later to have contact with two Anglican clergymen with academic backgrounds: the Reverend John Shulte, rector of Port Burwell and Vienna, and the Reverend J.P. Sheraton, principal of Wycliffe College. Shulte originally had been a Roman Catholic priest and was the first president of St. Francis Xavier College (later University) in Antigonish, Nova Scotia. Perhaps his influence on Wrong was responsible for the young man's later conversion from Methodism to Anglicanism. At Wycliffe College, Sheraton became the predominant influence.

Wycliffe, a very new college in the 1880s, had entered into its greatest period of vitality. Dedicated to Low Church Anglicanism, the halls were vibrant with evangelical fervour. Wrong, being a poor boy (there was a fund available for needy students) and eager to succeed, was very susceptible to such fervour. Habits learned at Wycliffe, such as rising before dawn for a day of hard work, stayed with him to the end. According to M.D. Meikle, the intellectual tone of Wycliffe when Wrong was both student and teacher was hostile to influences outside evangelical Protestantism. [1] Most secularizing trends of the previous fifty years were condemned as readily as popery. Yet some objective intellectual rigour was undoubtedly imparted to Wrong through Paxton Young's honours course in mental and moral philosophy, which he took at the nearby university. Wrong also travelled widely in the late 1880s.

It is difficult to know what weight to place upon these various influences on Wrong. As he was an Anglican minister with a deep commitment to community service, there was no question of his sincere, almost religious, devotion to his teaching duties. Yet he formed a close working association with Goldwin Smith whose Anglicanism had been broken in the classic Victorian crisis of faith. Perhaps his background of cultivated gentility and his life-long admiration of good manners made him at least apparently tolerant. While he taught at Wycliffe, Wrong increased his knowledge of history, religious studies, and languages. He also became a popular lecturer, even taking lessons from an actor to improve his technique.[2] In addition he had the good fortune to marry the daughter of Edward Blake, the Liberal leader, which widened both his interests and his circle of friends.

Wrong's inaugural lecture as professor of history at the University of Toronto in 1895 revealed no deep-seated philosophy of history. Such an attitude was in line with the traditional distrust of abstraction evident among English historians until the time of R.G. Collingwood in our own century. For Wrong, abstraction was linked to the propaganda associated with vague ideals, which usually led to folly.[3] Viewing human nature as unchanging, Wrong urged prolonged and patient observation of the past. As he stated:

> English political institutions show the firm balance derived from a deep historical setting. We have taken them from their home, and placed them amid conditions entirely different. Our society has had little of the stern discipline in political thinking of the firmly knit English society, and our want of this training makes us prone to follow abstract theories. But if modern experience teaches anything, it should be the futility of *doctrinaire* politics.[4]

Thus the indirect benefits of studying British constitutional history for a proper grasp of current Canadian developments were quite evident. Wrong also expressed anxiety about the place of history in the future university. In spite of Wrong's praise for his predecessor, it was clear that Wilson had not done much for the

discipline. Wrong was concerned not only that history had not advanced in relation to other university departments but that, when
compared to Europe, Canada had "no historical monuments relating to the events we study."[5] By that he meant that public interest
in history was of considerable importance to him and that in a
young nation one had to do much to work it up.

Unfortunately Wrong's acquisition of the chair of history was
traumatic. Though he had not been a history student, he had
taught ecclesiastical history at Wycliffe after 1883. Assisting
Goldwin Smith and working on his own book, *The Crusade of
1383*, had given him practical on-the-job training as a researcher.
And essentially Wrong had been the Toronto history department
after 1892, being its only lecturer following Wilson's departure.

However, students and faculty were quite indignant when they
learned of his elevation to the chair of history. Some years earlier
Sir Daniel Wilson had warned the Minister of Education about
charges of political patronage in, for example, the case of the recently appointed university librarian, who was a man of "no special aptitude to be a librarian."[6] Whether the advice was heeded or
not is unknown, but there was strong speculation that Wrong's appointment was due to the influence of his father-in-law, Edward
Blake, who also happened to be chancellor of the university. The
fact that Wrong was also paid almost double the normal salary for a
lecturer in his first year and his swift elevation to the rank of professor convinced many that these actions were academically in-
defensible and so the charge of political patronage was hurled at
the leaders of the university and provincial government.

Some student editorials claimed that the promotion had been
made after only fifteen minutes' deliberation, though several appli-
cations had been received. An irreverent article entitled "A Frag-

ment Found on the Lawn" claimed the successful applicant, "N. Umber Wunn," had received testimonials from "Say Little Esq., Publisher, Mr. Shall O'Brian of Timbuctoo, Africa, Professor Foss Hill N.G. of University of Nulla Bona and Nick Nack, Whalecatcher of Reikjavik, Greenland."[7] In a more serious tone the student newspaper, *The Varsity*, stated its case on 14 October 1894:

> The gentleman who received the appointment and who had held the position of lecturer for two years, is popular personally with the undergraduates. There is no one who knows him but esteems him highly as a Christian gentleman. For these reasons, we say, it is to be regretted that at the very outset of his professorial career, his usefulness should be undermined by the statements which are being bandied about the College from mouth to mouth and have even found their way to the press.

By the new year the charges were renewed by William Dale, a Toronto classics professor, in the *Globe* (9 February 1895). Dale was summarily dismissed by the university (actually the provincial government) for his public, unfounded accusations. Simultaneously, the editorial board of *The Varsity* was censured by the university administration for articles on Wrong and editor, J.A. Tucker, was suspended for his refusal to apologize. Further alleged threats by President James Loudon against *The Varsity* and charges of interference in the workings of the Political Science Club by the university council eventually provoked the famous students' strike of 1895. This consisted of a boycott of lectures following a mass meeting on 15 February.[8] While James Mavor, mem-

bers of the council, and others in authority incurred the wrath
of student protesters (including young William Lyon Mackenzie
King), Loudon took the brunt of it. He was even accused once of
turning tho hoee on a group of students.

A royal commission empowered to investigate the events leading
to the discipline question at Toronto found no fault in Blake and
dismissed accusations of political interference. Goldwin Smith,
however, in an interview with the university commissioners, urged
that government in future separate itself from the university so that
the issue of political interference could not be raised. But the main
cause of the unrest he determined to be the high schools, which
were graduating "a large number of students probably more democratic and less amenable to social rules."[9]

Wrong was exonerated in these matters and indeed had not been
a special target of strike leaders the way that the president had
been (though he had had one letter exchange in the press which he
later regretted). The two professors singled out for direct student
abuse had been Mavor of political economy and W.H. Van der
Smissen of the German department. Both were accused of being
poor teachers—Mavor's "manner and person" were said to be
"repellent," while Van der Smissen was accused of paying more
attention to women students and, on one occasion, guilty of repeat-
ing an entire lecture on Faust to the class of 1895! For Mavor, at
least, Smith had some sympathy, believing his Englishness had
made him the target of "nativist" antipathies.

For the first dozen years or so of Wrong's tenure no dramatic
changes occurred in the department as a whole. Possibly because
of the cloud hanging over the circumstances of his elevation, the
second professor applied himself with unusual diligence to the
everyday demands of teaching. Three years later he also founded

the *Review of Historical Publications Relating to Canada,* ancestor of *The Canadian Historical Review.* The *Review* was designed to foster historical work on Canada through critical scholarly reviews. Books were judged not only on their argumentation and quality of prose but also for their documentation. Thus emerged the two standard pillars for judgment of the modern discipline of history in this country: good teaching and research based upon original sources.

Wrong's approach to the study of history is interesting given his well-known admiration of Oxford. Even in his 1895 inaugural lecture he stated that "the first axiom of sound historical study is that it involves some, if necessarily a very limited, dealing with original authorities" (p 9). His interest in encouraging original research grew steadily thereafter, as we have seen. This was much the same approach as that of research professors at Oxford. Yet Wrong would also appear to have shared the pre-1914 Oxford tutors' view that history must train young men in the progressive values that would make them suited to be leaders of the civil service. In this Wrong was somewhat of a mediator between the two approaches.

Wrong's plan to build a department of many historians faced considerable problems. An early hurdle was the attitude of James Mavor. Their dispute concerned Wrong's attempt to move constitutional history from the Department of Political Economy to his own department. Mavor was a brilliant man equally committed to building his own academic empire and he believed that constitutional history had been bequeathed to political economy in Ashley's time. However, as W.D. Meikle has pointed out, constitutional history was the centre of Wrong's program of studies in the British Empire.[10] From this base it was easier to assimilate lecturers such as W.P.M. Kennedy who, as well as his substantial contributions to the British field, also wrote *The Constitution of*

Canada (1922). Mavor had other plans for the field as well as personal antipathy toward Wrong.

In time Wrong partly overcame Mavor by teaching the subject himself. After 1904 he also expanded the history staff. He thought that history should provide a vital service to Canada, developing character as well as a revitalized humanities program. W.J. Alexander of the English department was a friend of Wrong and helped him, thus preserving the older spirit of unity found in Wilson's time between history and literature. Wrong's sense of timing may also have reflected the public mood. Shortly after the expansion began, W.J. Ashley wrote to Wrong from England, observing that "if my impression—the impression of an outsider is correct: that the recent wave of economic prosperity in the Dominion has been accompanied by a new historical movement—the outcome of a strengthened national confidence and pride."[11]

Ashley may have been commenting upon both the growth of scholarship and of the nation. Wrong believed that proper teaching should be based on the tutorial system as well as lectures. In designing the honours course in history and the joint honours program in history and English, the tutorial system used at Oxford and Cambridge was used as the model. Such a system, of course, necessitated hiring more instructors, which Wrong did with great energy until there were eight department members. Ralph Hodder-Williams wrote in 1915 about the tutorial system that "It is a harder thing to give good tutorial classes to six students than good lectures to a hundred. To be ready to deal with any question that may arise, to brush aside 'red-herrings,' to draw out and to drive home again the points that tell, and to weld the interchanged ideas into an intelligible whole, is fit work for the most experienced. We must have more teachers, and they must be good teachers."[12]

While a department of eight does not seem large by today's standards, Toronto had achieved something of a breakthrough by the mid-1920s. At that time the largest history department in North America was Princeton, which had some twenty-one members, while universities such as Illinois and Stanford were about the same size as Toronto. In Canada most departments had from one to three members. The "research ideal," as A.B. McKillop has described it, had also been established at Toronto. [13]

Until 1919 history at McGill was in the hands of Charles W. Colby, the first Kingsford Professor, assisted by Charles Fryer, Vera Brown, and Stephen Leacock for a short period. Colby was a graduate of McGill who went on to obtain his PH.D. at Harvard. His return to McGill promised great things for the historical discipline. Though initially appointed in 1895 to teach both English and history, within the year he had been made professor of history. His primary interest was English history, in which he published *Selections from the Sources of English History* (1899). Later he published a number of works on New France and introduced Canadian history into the curriculum, though the latter was taught by his associates. But as Michael Perceval-Maxwell has concluded, Colby's was probably more of a negative than positive influence in the development of his department. [14] His frequent absences, some of which were connected with his presidency of the Noiseless Typewriter Company of New York, a rather dilettante approach to supervision of graduate theses, and perhaps his basic attitude toward the study of history were all to the detriment of his career. Colby wanted to popularize the teaching of history. He justified the latter position to some degree by his strong admonition that history must be well-written literature. [15] Perhaps, as Carl Berger has indicated, Colby ultimately digressed from the Rankean path because he thought that there could be no definitive history, each generation of historians being engaged in rewriting it for their contemporaries.[16] Such a position is reasonable but not one to inspire a crusade for research. In the end Colby chose typewriters over history.

McGill considered reorganizing and expanding its department in the 1920s. When the noted historian of eighteenth-century England, Basil Williams, began his tenure as head of the McGill department in 1921 he did a complete survey of its needs. The resulting report stressed that the small staff of three was overburdened and could not offer enough courses, make proper distinctions between honours and general students, and had no time for extensive reading or original research (denying the claim that "it is not the business of the professor to publish original research").[17]

In short, McGill under Williams wanted to take the same path as Toronto, and the excellence of Wrong's system was "a subject of envy." The tutorial system was thus deemed to be the best way to teach.

Williams was succeeded by William Templeton Waugh as Kingsford Professor in 1925. A student of medieval English history, Waugh had studied with the great T.F. Tout at Manchester. There he had been introduced to a system of training perhaps more rigorous than that at Oxford or Cambridge. Not only did Waugh publish books on the Middle Ages, but he was also interested in the English conquest of Canada and wrote a biography of James Wolfe (1928). His lecturing style was lively. On one occasion he did a rendition of "Summer is icumen in."

Not all early additions to the McGill staff were initially as well loved as Waugh. E.R. Adair, a Tudor historian who was to teach both British and Canadian history for decades, for much of his early career was thought to be difficult. Having been hired from London in 1925 he seems to have vanished to the south of France until the beginning of his first school year. Waugh noted in 1921 to Sir Arthur Currie, McGill's principal, that Adair's "behaviour is unusual to put it mildly."[18] In the years that followed, however, Adair supervised a large number of students and developed a strong interest in French Canada while maintaining his English historical pursuits.

In the West, former pupils of George Wrong began to build departments with the same goals as Toronto. At the University of Alberta, in Edmonton, G.S. Smith became head of the department in 1931, while at the University of Manitoba, in Winnipeg, Chester Martin instituted the teaching of history in a separate department in 1911. A Maritimer educated at Toronto and Oxford, Martin's interests embraced both British and Canadian constitutional history, mirroring to some degree the scope of his own imperial perspective. He was succeeded in 1928 by a thirty-year-old Englishman, Noel Fieldhouse. A former student described Fieldhouse at that time as "tall, very well-built, with a certain distinction in his bearing and a nice touch of not too-harmful arrogance hovering about his good looks."[19] Fieldhouse had been born in Sheffield and educated at Oxford, where he had befriended a classmate, A.J.P. Taylor. Under Fieldhouse, British history continued to be taught in reasonably large doses (about one-third of the courses) with the Victorian period being added by the war. While instructing and writing on the history of his homeland, especially its eighteenth-century history, Fieldhouse also focused upon other areas of European affairs such as diplomacy.

Eloquent as a lecturer, Fieldhouse nevertheless in his honours history sessions expected students to master basic facts themselves while he supplied them with numerous library references. As the eminent lawyer Maxwell Cohen remembered: "I had the temerity to choose Professor Fieldhouse for an honours course in which the procedure was a weekly meeting alone with him. To my astonishment I learned that I was expected to be ready each time with a paper and to show at least enough intelligence so as to discuss what I had read and written with a minimum of understanding.[20]

Cohen's observations on Fieldhouse's serious commitment to a quality honours program at Manitoba was born out in the latter's correspondence with the university administration. Urging that a clearer distinction be made between pass and honours students, Fieldhouse believed that "under the same roof within this degree-factory, we may then build a real University, in the shape of our Honours courses."[21] Fieldhouse believed it was necessary to limit the number of lectures in favour of the tutorial method. He also noted that limitations in the size of his faculty on the one hand and loose entrance standards on the other (as a non-endowed public institution) worked against this goal. As he stated with considerable conviction in the mid-thirties: "A professor should be free to give long hours of his time to those students who can profit from such contact with him, but in North America the great part of his energies have to be devoted to chasing large numbers of poor students over the same hurdle at the same time."[22]

Winnipeg also became an interesting place for those exposed to the wide views and influence of another historian of Britain (and later, of course, Canada), Arthur Lower at United College. By the 1950s United College had become noted for the vitality of its history professors and students, the British field by that time being taught by J.H.S. Reid and on occasion by Harry Crowe.

At the University of British Columbia in Vancouver the Department of History developed under Mack Eastman, who first taught in a department combined with economics and finally saw it become a separate entity after 1916. By the early 1920s the department also included Frank H. Soward and most particularly Walter Sage, who succeeded Eastman as head. Sage was Toronto's first PH.D. in history and taught in the British field. While admiring Britain, it was clear that he reacted against some earlier lines of British history writing which emphasized its Germanic roots as an explanation for Britain's success in government. Sage thought that this emphasis encouraged the idea of a chosen people. As he stated in a 1923 lecture, "let us shun this theory of History as we would the plague."[23] However, he had no doubt that Britain had made solid achievements in its constitution and that it was worthwhile for Canada to maintain its imperial links. Sage described Parliament as "the British Banyan tree in stone, and it proclaims the solidarity of the British world."

In Kingston, Queen's University had developed a department of three by the mid-1920s, first including J.L. Morrison, J.T. MacNeil, and A.E. Prince and later Duncan McArthur, Reginald Trotter, and Prince, who all taught aspects of British history as well as colonial, Canadian, and continental European history.

Trotter was well versed in his field, on occasion offering advice to friends about to teach British history elsewhere. MacArthur, on the other hand, was especially good at counselling students, including the young Gerald Graham, future Rhodes Professor of Imperial History at London.

At the University of Western Ontario, London, a variety of men taught history until after the Great War. We are fortunate in having the student notes of one of them, the distinguished historian, Fred

Landon, in the Western archives. Among other memorabilia are the course notes for C.B. Edwards' "Lectures on English Constitutional History 1905–6." The course reflected the usual Whig-Liberal emphasis on the importance of liberty and the "insular position" of Britain which had fostered an independent spirit.[24] The course also had the usual bias toward Protestantism, asserting that "growing intelligence and independence of the people was under the Reform movement."[25]

After 1920 Western came under the direction of Queen's-educated Arthur Garratt Dorland, who taught there for thirty-six years. Dorland could not rival the fifty-year span at Dalhousie of George Wilson, who was finally joined by Stanley Walker in teaching British history in the late 1930s.

At the small universities there were also advances in the discipline despite the Depression and other conditions imposing economic constraints. In the Maritimes, where the most small schools could be found, progress was clearly evident before 1939. Thomas Dadson, as well as R.S. Longley from time to time, taught British history at Acadia, in Wolfville, inspiring such figures as Donald Schurman and John Stewart to pursue graduate studies. Potentially less affluent St. Francis Xavier at Antigonish was helped by the contributed labour of its clergy at a time when full academic salaries would have imposed tremendous burdens. In 1920 an endowment campaign resulted in the collection of $470,000, but times were as hard for universities here as elsewhere by the Dirty Thirties. British history was taught by a variety of people, including the literary scholar, Father R.V. Bannon. Students benefited not only from his Harvard training but also from his travels to the British Isles. As he wrote to a fellow clergyman in July 1935:

Most of my time this summer has been spent in London, and I am not entirely "finished" with the metropolis, as yet. I have hiked the highways and bye-ways of that great city. I have tried to look at it under a microscope: I have tried to parse and analyse it! The literary shrines are often hidden, hard-to-find, or lost, *but* history is everywhere. This summer so far has proved a wonderful refresher course in English history for me.[26]

Father Bannon soon moved fully into the English department but British history continued to be taught principally by one of St. Francis Xavier's most famous teachers, Sister St. Veronica.

At Toronto the history department's move toward quality was certainly not made smoothly. Before the First World War University administrators made perhaps the worst decision on a teaching position in the annals of Canadian universities by rejecting the candidacy of a recent Oxford graduate. They spurned the application of one Mr. Bernstein, despite his first at Oxford, because of his eastern European background. It was felt that such a heritage would preclude a proper understanding of British institutions. The candidate was Lewis Bernstein Namier, later one of Britain's greatest historians![27]

On another occasion, however, Toronto showed great intelligence by hiring another Oxford graduate who was handicapped by blindness, Donald McDougall. Beginning life as a miner in northern Ontario, he had been blinded while serving with the Princess Patricia's Canadian Light Infantry in 1916. Having learned physiotherapy at St. Dunstan's Hospital while recovering from his wounds, McDougall returned to practise his craft at the Medical

Arts Building on St. George Street in Toronto. There he also in-
structed medical students in massage and from the proceeds paid
his way through the University of Toronto as a history student
(while also supporting his mother and sister). He completed the
four-year program in three years and obtained a Rhodes Foundation grant, being technically overage for the scholarship. Sir Roy
Wilson, a fellow Oxford student, remembered that "it was obvious
to all his friends that he had an exceptionally powerful, discerning
and well-stocked mind."[28] He took his final examinations in his
own rooms, typing up his answers while an invigilator stood by in
full academic regalia. He achieved a "scintillating" first.
McDougall's tutor, Humphrey Sumner, became a life-long friend.
Another of his Oxford teachers, Kenneth Bell (who spent some
time at Toronto), is rumoured also to have tutored C.M. MacInnes,
another blind Canadian who later became Professor of Imperial
History at Bristol.

Wrong's successor at Toronto, Chester Martin, thought that
McDougall would be unable to control students and so rejected his
first application to teach. But later McDougall accepted another
offer from Toronto, where he subsequently became renowned for
his teaching and overall mastery of the Tudor-Stuart field. As Mrs.
McDougall recalled:

> Donald was always determined to live as much like a
> sighted person as possible. In this he was successful up to
> the point that many people could hardly believe that he
> was totally blind. Besides...finding his way round the
> city, he amazed friends who came to the house by picking
> out gramophone records and books, and by the confident
> way he walked about the house. Apart from this, he was a

most efficient bed-maker and dish-washer, and no one else
was allowed to set and light the living room fire or to clear
it after use, as well as sawing up wood for it.[29]

McDougall's proficiency as a lecturer became legendary. He employed tricks of the trade, however. Many remembered how he
would pace the platform at times while giving lectures to large
classes, turning just before reaching the edge. He obviously had
measured the distance. It was a good attention-getter. Many remembered his ability to recite speeches of the great seemingly ver-
batim. But there were others at U of T capable of holding the attention of their students. Lester "Mike" Pearson, who taught British
history prior to McDougall's arrival, has also been described as
an interesting lecturer by C.P. Stacey, who noted his use of John
Drinkwater's play *Oliver Cromwell* instead of lecture notes on the
subject.[30] Nonetheless, McDougall's reputation as an orator was
unequalled.

Frank Underhill also joined the Toronto history faculty as part of
the contingent of Balliol-trained Canadians that Wrong hoped to
make the core of the department. Wrong argued in a letter to Underhill that the fixation upon Oxford training had a deeper purpose
to it. As he stated:

Oxford has moreover the advantage of being in the centre
of the modern state in which vast and pressing political
questions are in an acute state of discussion. The very effects of English life, the appalling poverty, the social injustice, the strength and tyranny of vested interests, make
its problems interesting. Here, where nearly every one is
tolerably comfortable, there is less interest and passion in

regard to contemporary questions. A man whose mind is
occupied with both Lloyd George and Aristotle is likely to
bring them together in his conversation.[31]

Certainly Wrong's idea bore fruit in Underhill's later career when
he also observed that history was "becoming more and more a history of political ideas."[32] As far as teaching British history was concerned, Underhill pursued his interests in the Labour party and
Fabianism in lectures, some publications, and a great many
reviews (which was also a way to keep up his supply of British
books). He tended to lecture on themes rather than employ the
chronological approach of textbooks. And he always had a pen-
chant for shocking his listeners. As he stated in an interview: "I
had one lecture I was very fond of, on Queen Victoria in her old
age, in which I surpassed myself in satire and so on and usually
one or two walked out, indignant—Toronto Tories—of my making
fun of the old Queen."[33]

In the 1930s the department also gained the services of Bertie
Wilkinson from Manchester. He joined Ralph Flenley and other
Englishmen, including Keith, later Sir Keith, Feiling, who taught
English history in conjunction with the Canadians who also lectured in the field. In all, British history, especially constitutional,
remained a mainstay of the department in spite of the infusion of
more teaching and writing about Canada. This was also the case
for most other departments in English Canada until the Second
World War.

While making tremendous strides toward professionalism, history had also become the source of extra-scholarly wisdom for
many undergraduates. Men such as Underhill, therefore, saw their
role as purveyors of ideas and attitudes far beyond our current and

narrower definition of an academic discipline. For many other professors throughout the country, history provided the key to unlock-
ing secrets of the Western world, thereby replacing classics. As
Sister St. Veronica regularly stated in her introduction to history
students at St. Francis Xavier, they were about to enter into the
"inheritance of culture."[34]

CHAPTER FOUR

NATION WARS AND EMPIRE

British historians in Canada were not disposed to retreat from public issues. Someone like George Wrong saw it as his duty to become engaged in the world beyond academe. Historians of Britain were well equipped to speak out on the principal issues of the day. Canada came of age between the 1890s, when most university history departments were established, and the end of the Second World War. This coming of age involved profound redefinitions of what it was to be Canadian. Were we to remain part of the British Empire? Were we to become part of a continental system with the United States? Whatever our external attachments, what about our Canadian identity? Canadian-British historians were by training and background well equipped to address these issues, though one might not have anticipated the wide range of views that would be expressed in the course of the discussion.

For Canadians there have always been many ways of expressing their identity or "Canadianism." As Carl Berger has demonstrated, some adherents of British imperialism in this country practised one form of Canadian nationalism.[1] As they saw it, Canada had been founded as a British nation and owed its continued existence to its connection with the Empire. Such Canadians saw no con tradiction between love of Canada and upholding the Empire. Anti-British sentiment stunted Canada, making it vulnerable to external threats. The American republic had ceased its military encroachments in the early nineteenth century, but it was still thought to be eyeing Canada as potential prey. Canada's survival therefore would be assured by continuance of the Empire. The cultural and philosophic links to Britain made imperialist attitudes far more than merely a matter of defence. To be Canadian and a British subject was not merely to be against the United States and all its influences. It was also a positive affirmation of what was right within our own society.

As the Victorian age was closing, some groups in both Canada and Britain hoped for even closer ties. Joseph Chamberlain, a Cabinet minister in Lord Salisbury's Conservative (Unionist) government, became a strong advocate of imperial federation. This was the notion that, for white colonial areas at least, closer ties should be maintained with Britain, including the fusion of economic systems through tariff protections, thus creating a sort of precursor to the European Common Market.

The idea of tariff protections had come up earlier in Canadian history with Sir John A. Macdonald's National Policy. Macdonald had asserted strongly that Canada was a British nation and had corresponded regularly with his fellow Conservative, Benjamin Disraeli, the original architect of the revived Empire. But neither Macdonald nor Disraeli conceived of a "Greater Britain" like the German Zollverein that would potentially stifle Canada's industrialization. Despite the inherent dangers in imperial federation, it had strong advocates in Canada and Chamberlain made a number of speeches in places such as Toronto about it.

Ironically, Goldwin Smith, although former Regius Professor of History at Oxford and an admirer of British civilization, was not an Empire man. His Liberal "Little Englandism" (anti-imperialist) bent led him almost inevitably to think that Canada and the United States should develop closer ties, the artificial continued emphasis of British-Canadian links benefitting neither side. In *Canada and the Canadian Question* (1891) he described the potential fruits of collaboration among all English-speaking peoples. Many years earlier Smith had been much criticized for advocating transformation of the Empire into a looser confederation of dominions. Yet he shared more in common with some imperialists than supposed, seeing the necessity of Anglo-Saxon unity in the world as a whole. Such a goal was not unlike Chamberlain's notion of a Teutonic alliance of Britain, the United States, and the German Empire.

Smith's fellow transplanted Englishman, William Ashley, held the opposite point of view. Though a staunch free trader while he was in England, Ashley underwent profound conversions not only in his religious convictions but also in his economic and political outlook. As mentioned earlier, he became an apostle of the German historical school of economics, renouncing the "Manchester school" of his youth. He also came to see great danger in laissez-faire policies with respect to Canada's destiny. In particular, Ashley became alarmed at the increasing economic influence of the United States. Eventually he became a social imperialist, advocating social reforms at home and support for the Empire abroad. In the process he endorsed Chamberlain's system of imperial preferences for the Empire as a way of combatting Canada's absorption by the United States.[2] For Ashley, part of his credo was that practical politics should complement scholarship.[3]

However, war brought the issues of nation and empire to full fruition in the twentieth century. The Boer War and the two world wars both accelerated social and political trends evident by the end of the nineteenth century and provided new twists and turns to Canadians' outlook on national affairs. Historians played a prominent role in this process.

The Boer War was the first event to elicit strong feelings by the founders of the historical profession in Canada. Goldwin Smith firmly opposed the war, shocked as much by the jingoism of Toronto as by that of his native Britain. He denounced in particular the churches (except the Baptists) for supporting the war.[4] Of course not all educated opinion in English Canada, certainly not in French Canada, supported the war. Roman Catholic schools, as T. Phillips Thompson noted, were conspicuous in *not* praising the war effort.[5] In eastern Canada it took a public lecture by Dr. D.M. MacGregor to convince some St. Francis Xavier University students that the pope was not anti-English after comments allegedly made by the local newspaper, *The Casket*. Such was the power of the lectern. As one student remarked, "After the Pope there was nobody in whom [he] had such confidence as Dr. MacGregor, and if the Doctor said the *Casket* was wrong, it must be wrong."[6] Goldwin Smith's position was as a harbinger of the independent outlook that characterized many historians in years to follow.

With George Wrong, however, one is confronted by the usual views of British institutions and the links of Empire. What was significant about him were his impressive efforts to wed scholarship to public debate. Smith had done so by holding court at The Grange, but as he was no longer a teacher and increasingly made journalism the centre of his life, he was outside day-to-day academe. Wrong, on the other hand, was at the very heart of university life, not only directing the routine operations of his department but also planning its destiny.

Wrong was an important member of the Round Table Movement in Canada, which flourished between 1909 and 1920. In association with Sir Robert Falconer, president of the university, Sir Joseph Flavelle, the university's businessman-benefactor, and Edward Kylie, a younger history department colleague, meetings and speeches were arranged which extolled the virtues of British civilization and the need for a closer political union within the Empire.[7] Much of this sentiment spilled over into Wrong's academic activity, not the least indication of which was the belief that an Oxford experience was the finishing touch to education. Young men were to have the right attitudes toward the nation and empire as part of their intellectual equipment, a sort of equivalent to the civic humanism of Renaissance times. Wrong saw the fruits of his work in students such as Chester Martin, who eventually succeeded him as history head at the University of Toronto.

The First World War and its aftermath brought more opportunities for public debate of these questions. A number of lecturers and would-be lecturers marched off to war and some, such as Toronto's Edward Kylie, didn't return. Most were extremely patriotic. As the uniformed Ralph Hodder-Williams wrote to George Wrong in 1915: "I believe your staff in Toronto preached the true gospel of our part in this war, and preached it long before August 1914, as nobody else in Canada has done, and from what I can see, few in England."[8]

The issues raised by Prime Minister Sir Robert Borden during the war and speculation about the future of the Empire following the Peace of Versailles led to more discussion of the Canadian-British relationship. Wrong had indicated his feelings about these matters in correspondence with men such as the Winnipeg journalist J.W. Dafoe, who also wanted "a permanent alliance of British nations dedicated to the cause of civilization and progress."[9]

Discussion of the nature of the empire was engaged in by such people as W.T. Waugh and E.R. Adair of McGill, Walter Sage of the University of British Columbia, and others. At this stage most of them supported the idea of a strong imperial connection. Canadian academics must have appeared to be very strong imperialists in the years immediately following the First World War. Dr. Clarence Perkins of Ohio State University, for example, applying for a position at Western in 1919, not only pointed to his publication of a textbook in English history but also made the following comments in his approach to this old Canadian school: "You may be interested to know that I am of purely English descent and that I have never at any time had any sympathy with the German world conquest plans. Having spent one year and several other summers in England, I cannot help liking the English people. In the course of several long visits to Canada, I have come to feel very friendly toward Canadians."[10]

By the 1930s some younger academics began to have second thoughts about the imperial connection, faced by the realities of the Depression, threats of renewed war in Europe, and the loosening of formal imperial ties by the Statute of Westminster (1931). Two such academics, both university teachers of British history, were to make their mark on the national stage at this time—Toronto's Frank Underhill and Arthur Lower of United College, Winnipeg.

Underhill, as we have seen, was a protégé of Wrong, imbibing a

mixture of "Lloyd George and Aristotle" at Balliol College, Oxford. This may well have been the making of Canada's most famous
intellectual gadfly, for originality in social and political thought
was not his strong point. In the interwar period, Underhill,
strongly influenced by British Leftists, had helped to organize the
Canadian Commonwealth Federation (CCF), and was the first president of the League for Social Reconstruction. He also wrote regularly for *The Canadian Forum*. But his admiration for British history and political ideas did not extend to the Baldwin-Chamberlain
government nor to automatic support for the Empire in international affairs. He had been critical of imperial federation even
while he was a student at Oxford, when the movement was in its
heyday.[11] Throughout the 1930s Underhill became increasingly vo-
cal about the need to distance Canada from British foreign policy
and was repeatedly warned by the provincial government and the
university administration to mend his ways. Underhill's encounters with premiers and university presidents are well
recounted in R. Douglas Francis's biography. Suffice it to say here
that Underhill almost lost his job in 1941 in one of the most celebrated cases of academic freedom in Canadian history. The attempted firing was the result of a much-publicized speech at the
Couchiching Conference (the annual meeting of the Canadian Institute of Public Affairs) in August 1940. The speech, not given
from a prepared text, was a realistic appraisal of Canada's new,
more natural position in the world, especially its relationship with
the United States, at the time of the Ogdensburg Agreement between Mackenzie King and Roosevelt. Unfortunately the timing of
the speech was poor, given the emotions following the outbreak of
war in Europe, and was deemed to be anti-British by much of the
public.

Donald Creighton, a colleague and an admirer of the traditional British connection (and an opponent of the continentalists), summed up his view of Underhill's later:

> For Underhill, true Canadian nationalism meant detachment and autonomy in Canada's relations with Great Britain and close association and co-operation in its relations with the United States. . . . No assertion of Canadian nationality against the British connection was ever described as "anti-British"; but all Canada's attempts to defend its freedom and integrity against the United States were invariably characterized as "anti-American."[12]

The attempt to fire Underhill in part reflected a longstanding lack of prudence by Underhill. President Cody's predecessor in office, Sir Robert Falconer, had written to Underhill early in his career about public perceptions of controversial views expressed by academics. Falconer, who had done much to further academic freedom, thought it was a sufficient triumph that academics be protected from reprisals when speaking about academic questions. This position might seem similar to that of theologians talking about exercising papal infallibility, but it was based on the legitimate fight to withdraw government influence in university life going back to Goldwin Smith's advice in the 1890s. Indeed, it was a cornerstone of the research ideal at the University of Toronto, something Wrong seemed to have overlooked. Underhill, though he had very different political views from Wrong, like Wrong mixed academic life with public life and bore the consequences. Falconer did not understand that academic freedom should protect professors who went beyond the academic to tilt at windmills.[13] Un-

derhill claimed to have been misquoted and was pilloried by politicians, university officials, and the press, but the essence of his
views had been well established already. He was not so very different in outlook from Arthur Lower. Certainly Lower maintained that
good relations with the United States were important and that links
with Britain were weakening, though he had a healthy respect for
the continuing strength of pro-British sentiment in Canada. As he
commented:

> My family was of a pretty conservative nature. Very typical
> English Canadian family, I think, in that we hardly knew
> the difference between Canada and England, it was all part
> of the same thing. It was only quite slowly, I think, that
> some concept of a country emerging and becoming a coun-
> try in its own right impinged on my consciousness. . . . But
> it was a slow process. And that is typical I think and
> normal for anybody brought up in one of the Dominions.[14]

Although the sense of nation was evolving, Lower feared that the
emotions resulting from participation in a new war on Britain's side
would again unleash "a spirit of ancestral kinship," as in the Boer
War and the First World War, making unity between French and
English Canadians impossible.[15] Lower believed the ties of Empire
were stronger than did Underhill, there being no war of independence in our history. As he stated: "We have never had any quar-
rel with our parent. The u.s. has, as we all know. They quarreled.
They went out and slammed the door, they turned around and
shoved their fist at the old man. We have never done anything like
that. I don't think even to this day that there is any suggestion of
animosity in the relationship."[16]

Underhill was not alone in feeling the fury of pro-British sentiment once war broke out. Noel Fieldhouse in Winnipeg had a similar shock (perhaps more so because of being British-born). Fieldhouse in the 1930s had become a prominent member of the Winnipeg branch of the Canadian Institute of International Affairs. Its
membership included Dafoe of the *Winnipeg Free Press* and Arthur
Lower. His experience in the CIIA was of singular importance to
Fieldhouse, who wrote later that the institute was the only activity
which made his intellectual and physical loneliness in Winnipeg
bearable.[17]

Maxwell Cohen believed that Fieldhouse moved the CIIA away
from its position prior to 1935, which had been essentially an old-
fashioned liberal view of cheery faith in the power of public opinion and the ability of the League of Nations to solve international
tensions. As he states: "It was Fieldhouse who, with epigram, incident and theory, very early in the thirties, insisted on an entirely
different premise, the premise of the power."[18] Fieldhouse's conservative critique also associated him with less popular positions
such as that of the French Right. Essentially he seemed to believe
that Britain's National Government either should have stopped op-
posing Germany and Italy or rearm. His acidic comments about
the fall of the capitalist economy in the Western world were
coupled with a belief that Fascism, with all its imperfections, was
at least attempting to supply a new social agenda for a beleaguered
society.[19] One can therefore understand the public reaction to his
speeches at the CIIA (once war had broken out) that, for example,
placed much of the responsibility for the fall of France on the British government. Such pronouncements were seen as anti-British.
As a petition signed by "A Few Canadians" and addressed to the

president of the university stated, "If you are a man, act, Canada has no room for traitorous rats."[20]

Such an outcry deeply offended Fieldhouse, who once stated in a letter to the president that he believed Germany now to be a poison to Europe and as alien as the Soviet Union.[21] But comments concerning Nazi Germany being more in line with the future in Europe did his cause little good inspite of his professed love of England.[22] Perhaps the essence of Fieldhouse's position can be found in the following sentence he wrote about the war: "I think England deserves to lose this war. . . but I want to be with Englishmen when they lose it."[23]

Once the war got going, of course, many academics rallied to the cause, historians of Britain being in the vanguard. Some, such as James Conacher, Maurice Careless, and David Spring, found themselves in uniform in defence and combat roles or eventually in the army's historical section in London. A special mobilization of thought and action also occurred on the home front. Outside the classroom this ranged from the daily editorial column in *The Halifax Chronicle* by Stanley Walker to more selective swipes at dictators. Bertie Wilkinson, resident in Canada since the late thirties, took up the cause of King and Empire in ways that may have surprised colleagues of earlier days. In reviewing Hitler's New Order speeches for the *University of Toronto Quarterly* in 1941, Wilkinson lamented the "frail defence" of popular education against Nazi propaganda and the need to fortify ourselves against "the possibility of such an attack, within the community, on our dignity and integrity."[24] By this time Wilkinson already had done much to combat the Fascist threat. In an early article he had argued for defence of the Empire if democracy was to survive. He believed that "the virtue has gone out of [the Canadian radical's] former opposition to the imperial connection as the source of all Canadian social and economic ills."[25]

Wilkinson did not confine himself to print. In his quest for unity and strength among Commonwealth members and the United States he directed the radio series "Stories from Canadian History." The series originally began in 1935 and was funded by Sydney Hermant, youthful President of Imperial Optical.[26] Hermant, a former Underhill student and president of the student council, was an Anglophile and a member of the Empire Club. Wilkinson revived the series and oversaw the production of new scripts based on a successful lecture series given by himself and Richard Saunders to evening students and visitors at the university. Wilkinson introduced the series on 17 September 1944. As he stated that Sunday evening:

> the picture of the slow evolution of our civilization through the centuries, of its immense sources of strength, is not only fascinating in itself, it is also the best safeguard of our generation against the short-cuts and facile promises which nearly wrecked the world in the period between the two great wars. One of the few good things to come out of the tragedy of this present struggle is the resurgence of old faiths and sources of inspiration in democratic countries.[27]

As it turned out, almost none of the broadcasts dealt with Canada, the bulk being drawn from British history. The pretext for this selection was to point to the roots of liberty and democratic institutions found in the European background to Canadian life, a view that logically would be held by a British constitutional historian. It also provided a rationale for a strong defence of Britain (and France) as the intellectual parents of the Dominion. Most of the lectures ended with an allusion to the contemporary struggle with the Fascists. Interestingly enough, a bow was again made to Cromwell in the old Whig-Liberal tradition: "Oliver has been called a dictator. In one sense he was a dictator, for his power was, ultimately, the power of the sword. But he was one of the least dictatorially minded dictators that history records."[28]

Propaganda could also affect the inner workings of university life. In 1940 the University of Toronto Senate and faculty had to decide how to deal with German students at the university. Some university officials insisted that all students should belong to the Canadian Officers' Training Corps and that German nationals ought not to be admitted as students. The colleges disagreed and argued about the obligation to instruct, which, of course, could also lead professors to other forms of propaganda.

One of the more interesting experiments of the war, also organized at Toronto, was a series of lectures delivered to German prisoners-of-war at Bowmanville and Gravenhurst. The lectures were given under the auspices of the International YMCA as a form of prisoners' aid. D. Jerome David of the YMCA and Herman Boeschenstein of the University College German department were the principal organizers of the lectures, which began in 1942 and were given initially by Toronto professor George Brown. Though the lectures concerned American history, as requested by the prisoners, British concepts of government shone through in discussion of such events as the American Revolution.[29] As a result, sufficient interest was developed in the differences between the American

and British forms of government to warrant attention on Britain
alone. Therefore in the winter of 1943–4 a series of lectures on
English constitutional history were given by Donald McDougall.
Dale R. Brown made the following report after hearing one of
McDougall's lectures in 1944:

> A short time ago I had the opportunity of escorting a blind
> professor from the University of Toronto to one of the
> camps. It was a thrill to sit in the midst of a group of 250
> German officers listening while he told about the begin-
> nings of the parliamentary form of government in England.
> The men listened closely to each word he had to say. When
> he had finished one of them leaned over to whisper in my
> ear, "That was excellent, wasn't it?"[30]

Both Brown and McDougall were quite pleased with the frequent questions the Germans asked after the lectures. At Bowmanville, McDougall gave a series of talks covering the whole span of
English history but focusing mainly on constitutional developments from the early Tudors to nineteenth-century parliamentary
reform. In the early lectures he stressed the antiquity of English
constitutional restraints on the power of kings. In his subsequent
report he noted particular interest on the part of the prisoners in
the rule of law, and 1688 revolutionary settlement, and the process
of evolution from the aristocratic constitution of the eighteenth
century to the democratic system in the years following the era of
reform (post-1832). At Gravenhurst he stated that "it was evident
that the interest of prisoners still centered about the career of
Oliver Cromwell and other aspects of the Puritan revolution. I was

questioned in particular upon the growth of the democratic movement during and after the Civil War."[31]

There is the question of whether all this was Allied propaganda
in the guise of history lectures, a violation of the spirit of the
Geneva convention. In response to this question it should be noted
that McDougall recorded in his report that "It was my special care
throughout to deal with this matter [limitations on head of state] as
far as possible in a descriptive way, and to avoid discussion of ab-
stract and speculative questions."[32]

Toward the end of his report McDougall also offered some advice to the committee:

> Informal discussion, in which prisoners of war would be
> permitted to ask questions, would, I think be an invaluable
> supplement to these lectures, and I should strongly recom-
> mend that every effort should be made to arrange for such
> discussion, at least for a short time, after each lecture.
> This is, of course, a more difficult matter than simply lec-
> turing to these prisoners, and the teacher who undertakes
> it must be more than ordinarily careful in dealing with any
> questions which may be asked. I had less experience in
> this method than my colleague who preceded me in Bow-
> manville, but my experience tends to confirm his opinion
> that questions were asked in good faith, that the prisoners
> were genuinely anxious for information, and that there was
> no desire on their part to engage in controversy. One pris-
> oner did remark, while walking to the gate after one of the
> lectures, that he should like to hear very much some com-
> parisons between British and modern German ideas of gov-

ernment, but he recognized at once, and himself said, that
this was, of course, impossible.[33]

The mobilization of Canadian universities in the war effort was impressive by any standard. For historians at home it involved not
only radio broadcasts to the public and lectures to prisoners-of-
war, but also the encouragement of officer training programs and
the like. Occasionally the university community could also be the
target of some emotionally tinged propaganda as from Queen's
British historian Eric Harrison: "Is it possible that murderous rape
such as this could be worked by the sub-human tools of Himmler
on the universities of Britain and America? Can it be imagined that
these booted gorillas could enter the women's colleges of Oxford,
St. Hilda's, Somerville, Lady Margaret Hall, or Newnham and
Girton, Cambridge?"[34]
    However, Harrison and others were equally articulate in making
dispassionate points about the importance of universities in preserving freedom of thought and the intellectual process of Western
civilization. As Harrison said eloquently about the teaching profession: "This present struggle is nothing new for the professors.
They have been at it for centuries. The reason for their long
engagement against tyranny is that their occupation with the fundamental problems of society is apt to make them acutely aware of
the issues at stake when liberty is threatened or denied."[35]
    The same sense of unity in the cause of King, Empire, freedom,
and democracy has not been rekindled since 1945. The more
muddled issues of the postwar world, the dissolution of the
Empire, Britain's own disinterest in old ties with the English-
speaking dominions eroded more clear-cut sentiments of the pe-

riod from 1939 to 1945. The issues raised by Lower and Underhill in the 1930s in hindsight seem to be more realistic. But sentiment for the old Empire and support for an ongoing cultural empire persisted well into the 1950s. This sentiment provided a stimulus and sometimes a challenge for historians in years to come.

In the postwar period historians continued to ponder issues involving Canadian identity. With the end of the Raj in India, the formal withdrawal of Eire, Burma, and other states from the Commonwealth, and Britain's weakening position as a world power, there seemed less and less reason to entertain strong imperialist hopes. Canada was truly a North American nation with only cultural and spiritual ties to the mother country. These ties continued to influence Canadians in many ways, of course. British books, films, and theatre were widely accepted. Many still thought studying in Britain was better than studying in the United States or in Canada. A cultural empire continued to exist and Canada took an active role in Commonwealth affairs. Even politicians tried to restore old ties, as in John G. Diefenbaker's attempt to massively increase trade with the United Kingdom in the late 1950s.

By the Trudeau era, the remnants of imperialist opposition to continentalism had been channelled into the anti-Americanism of the period. Donald Creighton exemplified an updated traditional hostility toward continentalism more commonly found in the late imperial period, which was distinct from the feelings of Trudeau Liberals about the dangers of American influence. In the meantime, the antipathy of the Canadian Left had been directed against the United States—creating a rather different situation from the public posture of an Underhill in the 1930s. Recently it has been Brian Mulroney's turn to unleash the old debate about

Canada's position in the Western world through the free trade
agreement with the United States. As in Goldwin Smith's day, the
discussion is heated and has stirred the feelings of historians as
well as everyone else. Unfortunately it seems that the public has
less interest in what our historians of Britain or Canada have to say
about the issue than in the past.

CHAPTER FIVE

THE VIEW FROM MORNINGSIDE HEIGHTS

J.B. Brebner (1895–1957) is well known to many as the author of some fine books in Canadian, especially Maritime, history. But there are many more sides to this distinguished Canadian academic. Brebner as a university professor was concerned mainly with teaching British history, a field in which he also made significant contributions. He was also intensely interested in the improvement of universities and advanced research in Canada. Like Frank Underhill he also believed the academic had a responsibility to speak out on issues wherever he could provide the public with useful insights.

What is fascinating is that Brebner was an expatriate who spent most of his entire professional life at Columbia University in New York City. An examination of Brebner's career can provide insight into a period of extreme importance in the development of the historical profession and of higher education in Canada. As one of a number of Canadian scholars working abroad at the time, Brebner is a conspicuous example of a portion of the Canadian intellectual community that has received remarkably little systematic attention.

Bartlet Brebner was born in Toronto in 1895. His father, James, was the well-known registrar of University College and the University of Toronto. "Jacobus Brebner" was inscribed inside all sheepskins and he prepared the university calendar for forty-three consecutive years; they were in turn nicknamed "Brebner Bibles."[1]

Bartlet Brebner studied at Jarvis Collegiate, the well-known school in the heart of old Toronto, and the University of Toronto Schools and entered University College in 1913 as an Edward Blake Scholar in classics and mathematics. His studies there were cut short in 1915, when he went to war. Eventually he received his BA, not at Toronto but at Oxford, and in modern history.

In 1921 Brebner joined the history department at Toronto where, in his own words, he taught everything "under the sun."[2] Much of his teaching, however, concerned Britain. The course list for 1923–4 shows that he lectured to second-year students on British history from 1485 to 1603 as well as had a section of a modern European course and group sessions on aspects of Canadian history.[3]

The reasons for Brebner's termination in 1925 are unclear. When he returned briefly to Oxford in 1925 to earn his B.Litt. degree, Wrong's son, Hume, was appointed to the department. Suspicions of nepotism were once again linked to George Wrong. Brebner, however, fortunately at that point secured a post at Columbia in New York, where he had taught a summer course two years earlier. His release from Toronto undoubtedly saddened his father James, who remained university registrar until 1930. Bartlet was also unhappy, as he had taken up teaching "in order to teach Canadians" and the prospect of any further impact on scholarship in his homeland must have seemed remote.[4]

There was no indication of any deep-seated animosity between Wrong and Brebner. Though Brebner was not a Balliol man, they had a mutual interest in research. Wrong's evangelical Anglican sense of mission was quite opposed to Brebner's sceptical nature, but both believed that the scholar had a responsibility to engage in public issues, including the defence of liberty. Obviously no hostile instructions were left by Wrong for his successor as chairman. In 1929 Brebner was offered a job at Toronto once again.[5]

Brebner, for his part, harboured no resentment toward George Wrong or Toronto. Almost thirty years after his release at Toronto, his entry for Wrong in the *Dictionary of National Biography (DNB)* was generous:

> G.M. Wrong was misleading because he lived through so much change in Canada and Canadian historiography and because of his superficial social snobbery. Yet, I hope I have indicated in a piece for the next DNB, his guiding intellectual criterion was excellence—American, British, or Canadian. Thus, although he "purged" me from Toronto as a "surplus" Canadian in 1924, he subsequently wrote me most interesting letters about my books, about American scholarship and his share in it, and about what he himself had had to contend with in Canada. We can let time obliterate the ephemeral in him and his work, for his enduring achievement after 1896 was very great.[6]

After his appointment to the Columbia faculty a number of Brebner's colleagues urged him to obtain a PH.D., now becoming the
more generally recognized credential for university teachers in the
United States. Some course requirements were waived and a thesis
topic was expeditiously arranged, leaving but one obstacle—the
PH.D. comprehensive examination board. The first question at the
oral examination directed at Brebner by the historical geographer
William R. Shepherd was "Where is Württemberg?" Brebner was
stumped. The remainder of the examination was a disaster and
Brebner was duly certified as having failed his PH.D. comprehensive examination.[7]

The story soon had a happy ending. With the production of his
thesis Brebner received his PH.D. in 1927 and by then had a reputation as an accomplished teacher. A university worksheet he
filled out in the 1930s indicates the wide range of teaching and administrative duties he performed in his early career. In eight years
of teaching he missed only an average of one day of class per year.[8]

The Columbia campus was not a totally alien environment for a
Canadian in the interwar years, some ground having been broken
there by James T. Shotwell early in the century, who went to
Columbia after studying history with Wrong at Toronto. At first
Shotwell had been afraid even to ask a policeman for directions
upon arriving in the city, "such was my fear of the corruption of the
New York police."[9] But after an initial struggle to survive, including a winter spent in an unheated room in Harlem, he adjusted
thoroughly to the environment. As he stated in "Some Reminiscences": "There I had found an intellectual home. I had a feeling
of definite comradeship with those great scholars, a privilege I
could not have enjoyed in Canada. There was nothing there to
compare with it."[10]

Shotwell subsequently went on to teach history at Columbia, write some eighteen books, become involved in United States commissions and conferences on international affairs from the Versailles Peace Conference onward (including the famous San Francisco conference of the UN in 1945), edit the 150-volume *Economic and Social History of World War I*, and become president of the Carnegie Endowment for International Peace. Interested in a paper read by Brebner on Canada in North American history in 1931, he persuaded the Carnegie Endowment to finance publication of a series of volumes on Canadian-American relations. Brebner was commissioned to write one volume. Later the political theorist Thomas Peardon, a Canadian interested in British history, became another of Brebner's colleagues at Columbia.

About the same time, life at Columbia inspired an interesting essay by Brebner for the *Columbia University Quarterly*. In this well-known piece Brebner compared academic life at the three universities he had known intimately—Toronto, Oxford, and Columbia. He indulged in some elaborate comparisons, such as when he described the student training at the three universities:

Oxford shares with Columbia the higher incidence of precocity, excels Toronto and Columbia in thoroughness, but does so in quite the narrowest area of intellectual application. Toronto lags in precocity, falls behind Oxford a little and surpasses Columbia by a good deal in thoroughness, and, while exhibiting less breadth than Columbia, considerably surpasses Oxford in that regard. Columbia approximately equals Oxford in precocity, falls behind the other two in thoroughness, but does so in a compromise with a greater breadth than either.[11]

Which environment Brebner favoured was difficult to say, for he made detailed comments about teaching methods and the like in all three. Clearly he was not disturbed by the fact that "New York rushes over, under and through" Columbia.[12] In the last resolve he saw the universities as not so very different, their differences being rooted in their local communities.

Brebner was busy in the late twenties and thirties churning out a variety of works relating to Canada and colonial history. His interest in economic history reflected that of Ashley and Brebner's own contemporaries such as Donald Creighton and Harold Innis. *New England's Outpost* (1927) focused on Acadia as a prize in the struggle between France and Britain. *Neutral Yankees of Nova Scotia* (1937) was the famous sequel to *New England's Outpost* and described developments in Nova Scotia until the end of the American Revolution and the colony's continuing quest for neutrality. The two books inspired further work in Maritime history, now a rich area of regional historical study in Canada.

Brebner obviously spent much time in archives in Ottawa and the Maritimes and remained closely in touch with Canadian historians. For a time he seemed to accept the opinion expressed by Lower, Underhill, and other continentalists that Canadian history could be conceived of purely in North American terms, though he did not write history in order to serve a political cause. Indeed, his own 1931 Canadian Historical Association paper and the Carnegie series on Canadian-American relations were based on this view. This period was also when he revised and completed Marcus Lee Hansen's *The Mingling of the Canadian and American Peoples* for publication (Yale University Press 1940).

By the time that book was published, however, Brebner had veered away from the continentalist view. Like his friends Harold

Innis and Gerald Graham, he saw that to leave Britain out in explaining Canadian history was a mistake. As Donald Creighton wrote "This assumption, he now recognized, was mistaken. North America could not be explained in purely North American terms. Canada in particular could not be understood without constant and copious reference to Europe in general and Great Britain in particular."[13]

One clue to Brebner's broader view could be seen in his essay "Oxford, Toronto and Columbia" where, while acknowledging that the notion of Canada as an interpreter between the United States and Britain had become a "platitude," he nonetheless saw such an assumption at work in the practical academic training of the Toronto staff.[14] His change of viewpoint may also have been the result of his Columbia teaching, which was mainly in the British area. One suspects it was even more the product of a dispassionate contemplation unmoved by emotions on either side of the issue.

Brebner worked on bits and pieces of what perhaps would be his greatest work, *The North Atlantic Triangle*, throughout the late 1930s. In that period he began to move away from the frontier thesis (he confessed that he didn't actually read Frederick Jackson Turner's work until 1940) toward the ideas of J.A. Williamson and others at Columbia on the expansion of Europe.[15] His synthetic work, *The Explorers of North America* (1932), was a by-product of some of this intellectual background. His article for the Wrong collection published in 1939 revealed his new thinking on the subject.[16]

The outbreak of the Second World War had a profound effect on Brebner. By 1943 he had to rethink the whole final form of *The North Atlantic Triangle*.[17] Paradoxically, while Britain seemed to recede in the thinking of historians such as Underhill, for Brebner

it became more important. There was also his own attitude toward
the war effort. Although not a Round Table man, he seemed to
have a sincere attachment to the Empire. He was also quite concerned about appeasement and the general state of affairs in
Europe. In a letter to J.W. Dafoe in the late thirties, Brebner indicated that both he and Shotwell were discouraged by British and
French foreign policy.[18] At the outset of the war, Brebner was not
pleased about American neutrality. The 1940 presidential election
campaign left him cold, and as he confessed in a letter to a British
colleague, "your prospects of a working democracy are, at the moment, better than ours."[19]

The Underhill affair in 1941 also deeply distressed him. When
Underhill contacted Brebner about his dismissal from the University of Toronto, Brebner instantly replied with a telegram to the
university's board of governors urging reinstatement. There was
more than merely collegial support in his action. As he stated in a
letter to Harold Innis:

> I am distressed to hear that Underhill is under fire and in
> danger of dismissal and I am wondering whether there is
> much general recognition in Toronto of how serious an ef-
> fect that would have down here. In influential circles
> American admiration for Great Britain is habitually con-
> nected with the contrast between public expression in the
> British Isles and under the dictatorships. Already Amer-
> ican periodicals have made a certain amount of capital out
> of Canadian restraints on public expression, and anti-
> British groups have pointed to Canada in support of their
> allegations that the British can be as dictatorial as any-
> one. ... Is this a time, then, to allow a Toronto professor

to be forced out for exercising the ordinary rights of a British citizen?[20]

Brebner also noted that the timing of this persecution for "the sin of being pro-American" was ill-fated given Lord Halifax's (the British Foreign Secretary) mission to the United States within a few days. Of Brebner's personal commitment to the British-Canadian side in the war there can be little doubt. When asked to accept the Kingsford Chair of History by Principal Cyril James of McGill in the spring of 1941, he declined, pointing out, among other things, that "my closest colleague here has done much to persuade me that in the difficult period of Canadian-American relations which necessarily lies ahead I can be of greater usefulness in the United States than in Canada."[21]

After Pearl Harbor, Brebner became a staunch supporter of the American war effort. In 1942 he approved scripts for five programs on Canada as part of the series "Lands of the Free" broadcast by NBC radio.[22] He declined an offer to work for the State Department (he was by then an American citizen), but he did engage in an interesting project, which was both a piece of scholarship and an aid to the Allied cause, by writing *The Making of Modern Britain*. Brebner described his effort to Innis as follows in 1943: "I am on the last lap of a piece of folly, namely writing a 50,000 word history of Great Britain in the spare time of 2½ months. A number of American and British agencies of one sort or another combined to ask for it and it seemed the only war job for which I had any competence."[23]

Actually the purposes of this book were somewhat loftier. In the early part of the war it became obvious that American servicemen would have to learn more about the customs and traditions of their host and ally. The theme of books "playing a part in winning the war" had been raised by the American publisher Curtice Hitchcock at a Mansion House speech to a group of American and British publishers in November 1942. At the same London meeting Brendan Bracken, the British Minister of Information, had suggested the publication of a "wise" history of the United States for English readers and had urged that a similar British history be produced by American publishers. Many prominent people supported these endeavours, including T.S. Eliot, Rebecca West, and in particular William Temple, Archbishop of Canterbury.[24] About this time Brebner had been contacted by the Council of Books in Wartime to provide a short "wise" history for the United States armed forces. He was open to the call.

As Brebner later remarked, the book took only ten weeks to produce during the teaching year.[25] Allan Nevins wrote an introductory chapter explaining the significance of British history (he had earlier written an American history for English schools) and Brebner did the rest.

There were a few snags along the way, not the least of which was choosing a title. The publisher, W.W. Norton of New York, also suggested that one of the chapter titles be changed from "Birth of a Nation," thinking that Americans might confuse it with the famous D.W. Griffiths film.[26] Some 50,000 copies were printed per month over the next year, reaching 82,000 per month in early 1944, at a time when Yale University Press had insufficient paper to produce *The North Atlantic Triangle*.

The Making of Modern Britain received excellent reviews. Brebner's preface stated that it was important for Americans to know more about British history, "more of the magnificent drama and adventure bound up in the record, and of its cardinal significance in the story of humanity's slow advance towards liberty and tolerance."[27] He had much to say about the "borrowings" of institutions and practices of law and justice from Britain used in the United States as well as cultural and philanthropic traditions. There was a surprisingly dense textual quality to a manuscript written so quickly. Apart from a volume in the Home University Library series published by the Henry Holt Company, there was nothing quite like it for the general American readership. According to Jacques Barzun in the *Herald Tribune Weekly Book Review* (25 July 1943), Brebner had not only achieved "a brilliant feat of condensation" but had written history, not propaganda: "For in Brebner's pages the making of Britain is not a gorgeous pageant ruled by unfailing courtesy and good sense. It is history, that is to say, a chaotic mess, full of error and injustice, folly and false starts, but at the same time it is human history; that is, a tale in which can be discerned intelligible purpose, reason, inspiration and successes worthy of praise."

Others, of course, praised its readability and lack of dullness. As far as its basic purpose went the *Los Angeles Times* review by Paul Jordan-Smith stated: "If our fighting men want to understand why the British are what they are, why they prize their liberties and have survived their blunders; if our homefolk want a brief but authoritative resumé of the most significant phases of British history, this is the book" (4 July 1943).

Outside the United States interest was expressed as far away as New Zealand and plans were entertained for Spanish and Portuguese translations. What is particularly interesting was the enthusiastic British response. *The Observer* stated: "The book has the honest frankness of the New World backed by a scholar's equipment. It comes across the Atlantic charged with healthy sea air."[28] Individual English readers claimed a "better proportioned view" to be found in the pages of a text written by a North American. A British lieutenant in Manchester wrote that "your work is easily the most complete short history of my own country that I have ever read."[29] Much to Brebner's surprise, Unwin planned a British edition of the book, which had never been intended for a British audience. As Brebner said, "it is good to know too that Unwin wants to bring out a British edition. It may be that Britons nowadays are interested in reading what other people think of their history."[30] Again shades of *The North Atlantic Triangle* were intruding into his own life. His British profits were to be donated to St. Dunstan's Hospital, the famous soldiers' hospital where Donald McDougall and others had been rehabilitated in the First World War.

In relation to the primary, original market—the armed forces—by the spring of 1944 Norton was writing to Brebner to inform him that it was unlikely that the book would be reissued. Norton's reasons were based on an assessment of the political attitudes which might affect Army decisions. In particular it seemed that there was hostility toward Allan Nevins by at least one Congressman.[31]

After the war, Brebner's own scholarly interests were increasingly in British history. This occurred at the very time that *The North Atlantic Triangle* was finally published. This long-awaited contribution to the Carnegie series on Canadian-American relations paradoxically gave renewed emphasis to Britain's influence on Canada. As Brebner wrote to Maurice Careless in the mid-1950s concerning the convoluted direction of his research: "There is one moral to this autobiography. In 1921 I decided that I would not dare study either Canadian-American relations or the industrialization of Britain because of the complexity of both."[32]

Brebner's greater attention to British history was due to a variety of circumstances. His main area of teaching always had been British, as his copious notes attest. Upon succeeding Robert L. Schuyler as Gouverneur Morris Professor of History at Columbia, he conducted a graduate seminar in modern British history. This coincided with renewed, trans-atlantic interest in Victorian Britain. Brebner's seminar shared the honour with that of David Owen at Harvard and Kitson Clark at Cambridge of spearheading scholarly work in the field. Among his PH.D. students were R.K. Webb, Bernard Semmel, Emmet Larkin, and Olive Brose, all of whom made significant contributions to modern English, Irish, and imperial history.

Brebner's teaching style was distinctive. He was not a showy performer and shunned visual aids including the blackboard. He was invariably seated when lecturing. Emmet Larkin remembered that he was "very well organized and kept the attention by the force of his ideas rather than by the more artful devices sometimes used by teachers."[33] Senator John Stewart recalls that Brebner's lectures were fascinating, conveying a flavour of the period under consideration.[34] All his former students interviewed corroborate the systematic, highly organized nature of his presentations.

Brebner's graduate seminar was also meticulously ordered according to former students. Again seated, usually with folders placed before him, he played a low-key supervisory role and was kindly encouraging. He was serious in his manner, if not grave. Larkin remembers his humour as "always dry and often a little ironic."[35]

Both in undergraduate and graduate teaching Brebner made imaginative use of original sources, frequently quoting from documents. Much of this came from material gathered for a projected multi-volume history of industrial England (the other area besides Canadian-American relations he vowed not to tackle in 1921), which, alas, was incomplete when he died in 1957. He supervised a wide range of topics, usually guiding students toward a general subject area and then letting them do it their own way. Bernard Semmel remembers Brebner providing helpful warnings on general topic areas that might be unfruitful.[36] Toward the end of the dissertation Brebner would provide many pages of elaborate and detailed criticisms. Larkin believed that "his great virtue in criticizing my history was that he had exquisite taste, and very little that was gauche escaped his eye."[37]

Most former students remember his wonderful talents as an examiner, whether for comprehensive examinations or dissertations —fair, unthreatening, and yet formidable. His students have developed a wide range of intellectual interests. Ping-Ti Ho, for example, now the distinguished professor of Chinese history at Chicago, completed a thesis in imperial history under Brebner. As W.S. McNutt once commented, using a phrase said of Burke, "his mind roamed the universe."[38]

Brebner, like Donald Creighton, saw history as a work of literature. Hence high standards of writing were to be observed. R.K. Webb remembers some special words of advice: after completing a manuscript always redo the first and last paragraphs; avoid "and" in a title (it connotes a muddled idea of what the subject is about).[39] In the last resolve, reflecting his own writings, Brebner believed that the historian must synthesize all factors of explanation.

Specific topic areas did not escape his concern. *The North Atlantic Triangle*, like his earlier Maritime books, contained copious detail as well as general synthesis, much of it in the economic area. Indeed, Brebner's close relationship with Harold Innis served him well in this respect. His one specialized piece of British scholarship turned out to be singularly important. In 1948 he delivered a paper on "Laissez-Faire and State Intervention in Nineteenth-Century Britain" that was subsequently published in *The Journal of Economic History*. In the article Brebner pointed to the many forms of state intervention which took place in an era when free enterprise rhetoric was prevalent. He also took a very different interpretation of Benthamism from that traditionally espoused by A.V. Dicey and his disciples. Brebner, in many respects, initiated the avalanche of books and articles in the fifties, sixties, and seventies on the "administrative revolution" question and Bentham. Some of the material was derived from notes collected for his history of industrial England.

Brebner also contributed an insightful piece on the great French historian of England, Elie Halévy, for the essays in honour of R.L. Schuyler published in 1951 (*Some Modern Historians of Britain*, edited by Herman Ausubel, J.B. Brebner, and Erling M. Hunt). He was personally acquainted with Halévy and did much to promote the reading of his works in the English-speaking world.[40] He admired the Frenchman's dispassionate, "outsider" approach to the complexities of English history, a quality he shared. An interesting fact about Brebner's students is that at least three have produced major works on the role of religion in modern English history. Here, indirectly, the influence of Halévy may be seen. In the course of interviews for this book, none of Brebner's former students recalled particular emphasis being placed on religion in Brebner's lectures or seminars, though Bernard Semmel noted "his passionate devotion to oddity"[41] which could turn people toward areas not previously emphasized. At that time religion's role in history was not a particularly popular subject.

Brebner's good friend Gerald Graham noted his fascination with anything and everything. According to Graham, when Brebner was visiting Pitt Professor at Cambridge in the mid-1950s some of his friends played a trick on him. They invented a fictitious species of deer and discretely introduced it into common room conversation when he was present. As a result, Brebner for some time was worried and perplexed about this apparently sizeable gap in his knowledge. [42]

It was just as well that Brebner could analyse all immediate situations, for he was often thrust into troubled waters. Though a naturalized American citizen, he was not deeply involved with politics. After the Second World War, however, he was struck by the need for the United States to assume responsible world leadership. In a 1948 speech to a Columbia alumni meeting entitled "The Contracting British Empire: Its Meaning for America," he was quick to point out misleading analogies to Victorian Britain for present-day American statesmen. In the area of economics, he explained that Britain "paid the world for most of its raw materials in exchange for finished goods" whereas the United States had acquired "indebtedness from other nations."[43] He also chided the U.S. for its increasingly large defence budgets, noting that "Britain conveyed the impression of being fearless, although it was not. Now the rest of the world finds us inexplicably frightened, and we add to the impression by behaving like a rich man who, caught in a poor group, is willing to pay for protection."

In a speech to the English-Speaking Union on "The Democratic Foundations of Government" in the same year, 1948, Brebner again warned against the strains of rearmament. While discussing the various traditional checks upon authoritarian government in Britain, he noted that the country was reasonably well governed by the Labour party, providing that massive rearmament did not occur—"herein lies Britain's greatest economic vulnerability."[44] According to Brebner, if too great a proportion of the national income went to armaments, "the now insulated, dangerous ideas will infiltrate and destroy the prevailing climate of opinion in Britain. Her austerity program and her enterprise will disintegrate. Divisions, schisms, even chasms will result, and Great Britain may possibly find herself suffering from the same dangerous inertia which defeated France in 1939 and 1940."[45] The United States could draw the necessary conclusion, for it could not maintain the peace "as cheaply—in proportion to national income—as Great Britain in the 19th century."

Such views did not endear him in certain circles. Brebner also lamented aspects of the emerging Cold War, referring to Churchill's "unfortunate image of the Iron Curtain." As he stated to the Society of Older Graduates of Columbia on 16 April 1947:

It seems probable that if all of us here were to search around among our thoughts and feelings in order to find the largest single container for our present disquiets and forebodings, the majority might agree that it was not nuclear energy, but the popular fallacy of the Two Worlds—West *versus* East, Capitalism *versus* Socialism, Democracy *versus* Despotism, Individualism *versus* Collectivism, or any other metaphor for these habitual, absolute, polar opposites. After our happy intoxication from the repeated toasts to one World which alliance in war toward one objective quite truly justified, we are sunk in a morning-after hang-over and convinced that we have disposed of one enemy only to create another. We are tired, and rightly so. We have an

immense amount of repair work to do, not only for ourselves and our recent friends, but also our late enemies.
Whenever we are thwarted, whenever we discover that our
reach exceeds our grasp, we clasp our aching heads and
blame it all on those Russians.[46]

Unfortunately, the times were not conducive to dispassionate
analysis—the age of Senator Joe McCarthy was at hand. In 1949
direct communication with J. Edgar Hoover in an investigation of a
former student working for the Canadian Department of External
Affairs caused "puzzlement" in Brebner.[47] The next year one of
Brebner's Canadian PH.D. students missed his comprehensive examination when he was taken off the train at the American border
and subjected to a lengthy interrogation about his political ideas.
The student, who proclaimed his anti-Communism, worried about
his new academic employer's reaction.[48] The student was Harry
Crowe, who became the principal victim in one of the most celebrated academic freedom cases of the 1950s at United College,
Winnipeg. This border affair and Crowe's subsequent troubles,
however, seem to be unrelated.

For Brebner himself the anti-Communist crusade soon hit in full
force. In 1952 it was disclosed that Senator Richard Nixon had accepted an expense fund of $18,235 from a group of California
businessmen to help finance his vice-presidential campaign. As
the Republican presidential candidate, Dwight Eisenhower, was
then president of the university, many of the Columbia faculty
were quite interested in the issue. There was certainly political
bias against the Republican ticket among some Democratically-
inclined faculty supporters of the original "egghead"—Adlai
Stevenson of Illinois. Brebner himself, according to Semmel, had

once had a discouraging exchange of views with Eisenhower as they were awaiting a convocation ceremony. In any case twenty-three Columbia professors, Brebner included, publicly questioned Nixon's morals. Nixon successfully defended himself against the charge of being a tool of special interest in his famous television "checkers speech," but more trouble with Nixon supporters would follow.

Since the Alger Hiss case and his early Congressional campaigns, Nixon had commanded the respect of the "Cold Warriors." Hence when the Columbia faculty questioned his morals, his friends hit back with a story in the *New York Daily News* (9 October 1952), calling nine of the professors "Pinkos." Brebner's photograph made the front page, along with Henry Steele Commager, Mark Van Doren, and Robert MacIver. There were said to be files on all the academics maintained by the House Un-American Affairs Committee. Brebner was specifically cited as being a member of the technical and advisory staff of an American trade union delegation to the USSR in 1927. Benjamin Gitlow, former secretary-general of the U.S. Communist party, allegedly testified that all the staff were "party people."

Brebner's response was swift and to the point. In a letter to the editor of the *Daily News* he denied being a Communist, pointing out: "I went to Russia in 1927 and paid my own way so as not to be obligated to anyone. I did not share in writing the report of the trade union delegation. The historical question that I was interested in at that time, namely the relationship between the government and the peasants, was answered almost immediately afterwards by the well-known roundup and exile of the Kulaks."[49] Brebner may well have been part of the famous delegation, along with H.G. Wells, that met Stalin. In any case the newspaper battle was

resolved, but not without the untimely misfortune of being linked
with Communism. Former students recall a weekend in the country in which Brebner referred rather frequently to being called a
"Pinko."

There was much irony in the accusation of Brebner's being af-
filiated with Communism. Thomas Lamont in *The Saturday Review*
had thought that *The Making of Modern Britain* showed "some of
our Leftists" a better pattern for progress "through generations of
civil liberty and political freedom."[50] Later *Voprosy istorii*, published by the Soviet Academy of Sciences, ended a review of *The
North Atlantic Triangle* as follows: "Brebner's book, which propa-
gates the idea of reproachment between Canada and the United
States and of co-operation with Great Britain under the hegemony
of the United States, is the most conspicuous instance of how the
quasi-science of history serves exclusively as a tool of American
monopolies."[51]

In 1954, soon after the "Pinko" episode and not long before his
death, Brebner was asked to give the bicentennial university convocation address at the Cathedral of St. John the Divine in New
York. This great honour indicated the general respect the Columbia faculty had for him. The speech was entitled "Humility" and
summed up what Brebner thought the scholar's role in society
should be. It also says a lot about the man who delivered it:

> During recent years, a hurricane of investigations and per-
> secutions has lashed those parts of the earth where men in
> political authority have conceived themselves to be com-
> pelled to maintain one set of values and to attack all
> others. Throughout these operations, nothing has been
> more dreadful than the common assumption that every man

must at all times be "right." Surely this intolerance of vari-
ation is hubris—the insolent vainglory and self-assurance
that the Greeks denominated the basic, the suicidal, sin.
In our time this sin may take the form of worshiping the
power over nature or over human nature or the deification
of a man, an economic entity, a political party or a nation
state.

We academic persons know better than this—indeed,
true scholars are by nature humble—but many of us forget
that non-academic persons know better, too. Each group,
they and we, is largely to blame for being misunderstood,
and therefore for being mistrusted, by the other. Let us
then, for our part, exalt and extend our knowledge by all
means, but let us also constantly assert our uncertainties,
our ambiguities, and therefore our eternal need to know
and to think more. If we do so, it seems likely that non-
academic persons will be quick to recognize that we and
they are similar individuals, in the same boat on perilous
waters, and that they will the more trustingly pool their
skills with ours in guiding its voyage.

Scholarship, that is to say, the most perfected form of
knowledge, is non-academic as well as academic. Both
kinds of true scholarship are humble and inquiring.
Humility is man's best common ground. If that ground is
properly surveyed and delineated, it seems reasonable to
believe that there will be fewer attempts to impose limits
on man's right to knowledge and its use.

And, finally, through humility we might expect to regain
the salutary sense of the absurdity of man, laugh a little
more at ourselves, and be better prepared for being

laughed at. If we could thus offset our sense of doom, and restore the balance of the comic and the tragic that is man's fate, it is at least conceivable that our poets, our prophets and our other artists might flourish in communion with a broader and a more appreciative public than they have recently been able to enlist.[52]

Despite his claim to Careless that he hadn't done anything in Canadian history "worth mentioning" since 1944, Brebner's interest in his homeland remained constant. *The North Atlantic Triangle* was extremely well received. Since then it has produced academic cottage industries of various sorts, including works by historians such as George Rawlyk who refute some of its conclusions.

Brebner's last remaining work on Canada of any significance, a textbook entitled *Canada: A Modern History,* was published three years after his death. Brebner was unwell while he was writing it, so the University of Michigan Press asked the British and Canadian historian at Bishop's, D.C. Masters, to complete the manuscript. Masters had criticized some of the manuscript earlier, at Brebner's request. Later he wrote the final chapter and saw it through the press. Masters' memory of Brebner was of a kindly, established scholar who was always cordial to the young and uninfluential, unlike many who in earlier days had tried to keep the Canadian Historical Association small and exclusive.[53] The response to the book was not uniformly positive, but a second edition was issued in 1970.

Some historians may have concluded that Brebner in his late period viewed Canada through American eyes even though he was considered far more objective and "scientific" than many of his

Canadian contemporaries. Otherwise, as George Rawlyk has indicated, Brebner's main research was on the Maritimes in its pre-
Confederation days and therefore was hard to integrate into the
prevalent, central Canadian notions of what was seen as
mainstream Canadian history.[54] But no one could deny that in his
original research Brebner had been extremely interested in the
ideas and reactions of Canadian historians, particularly those in
the Maritimes.

Although he was not continuously engaged in writing Canadian
history, Brebner's ties with Canada remained strong. In 1944 he
made three Canadian trips: one to Nova Scotia and New Brunswick
in February, another to the Canadian West from March to May,
and a third in July to northern Ontario and Quebec. In relation to
his western trip he noted that there were two underlying aims: "(a)
Acquaintance with a part of North America which I did not know
sufficiently well for professional purposes and (b) Investigations of
the interplay between the United States and Canada in that
region."[55] He typed up reports recounting in great detail the economic, political, and cultural life of all three areas visited,
presumably for his own enrichment as well as for the Rockefeller
Foundation, again indicating an intellect constantly in motion.

In his Maritime tour Brebner took careful note of the negative
effect of Lord Halifax's January speech in Toronto on the need for
central direction in the British Commonwealth. Here he was interested in the confused reactions stemming from isolationist Canadian nationalism of the interwar period and "instinctive imperialism and loyalty to Britain," which were "natural outgrowths
of their role in Britain's wars for two hundred years."[56] By the end
of February, however, "there were signs of a third stage—i.e. of a
compromise between the isolationist Canadian nationalism which

took such firm root between 1918 and 1938 and plans for association with Great Britain and the United States, or both, or most desirably, with a world association of nations."[57]

Some of Brebner's observations were also very regional. He noted that the migration of young Maritime workers had already shifted in the direction of central Canada, away from New England. He wisely observed that efforts to Anglicize the Acadians would fail, criticizing in the process some wealthy St. John English-speaking leaders who during the 1941 conscription referendum had suggested that a tolerable way of solving French isolationism would be to join the United States.[58]

On the linguistic question he commented that the Moncton area was "a sort of urban battle-ground" with the English-speaking Protestants becoming a minority, though one that retained much of the wealth. However, he held out some hope for compromise elsewhere in the Maritimes, especially among Acadians, Scots, and Irish, most of whom were Roman Catholic.

Brebner spent considerable time visiting Canadian universities. For example, he gave the Founders' Day address on the "Uses and Abuses of History" at the University of New Brunswick during his 1944 trip. However, he was often harsh in his comments on university life: "The so-called 'universities' of the Maritimes, except Dalhousie at Halifax, do not deserve the name, for they represent only modest evolution from the old Academy and College combination and all of them are in such financial straits that they cannot afford to purge their student bodies."[59]

In such sweeping, general views Brebner did betray an "élitist" view of higher education, though this was not uncharacteristic of academics with backgrounds like his. However, he discerned important differences among schools. The student body of St. Francis Xavier exhibited "extraordinary vigour" and upon asking students of their opinions on current affairs Brebner received "a rapid fire of answers which rather surprised the reverend fathers and me by their focus in social and economic change, in a sense of Canadian nationality, and in awareness of international relations."[60] At Mount Allison he found the School of Fine Arts to be "a somewhat unexpected and quite vigorous institution."[61] He gave stern advice on occasion. For New Brunswick he said: "since Fredericton is the Provincial Capital, the ordinary tension Between Town and Gown carries over perceptibly to the Legislature which ought to be giving UNB more vigorous attention and support."[62] Acadia was found to reflect "discouragingly the smug conservatism of wealthy King's and Annapolis Counties," and he advised that the university needed "a courageous and progressive President who will worry less about business deals and more about the quality of his staff and students."[63]

Brebner's tours and judgments on various Maritime universities undoubtedly had a bearing on his book *Scholarship for Canada: The Function of Graduate Studies* (Ottawa 1945), produced for the Canadian Social Science Research Council. Certainly élitism emerged again for, as he stated, "higher education is by nature aristocratic, not in terms of wealth, but of brains..." (p 28). Like Wrong, he advised the careful sifting of students into honours programs and even further gradations within them! Instruction, Brebner thought, increasingly should be to small groups of less than twenty-five with previous reading required of students before discussion. The set lecture should be abandoned and so should large classes where "teachers have to be entertainers in order to attract and hold audiences..." (p 28). One can imagine what Brebner's attitude would be toward the mass lectures and student evaluations of the seventies.

To effect these changes, universities would need more and better paid staff. Sabbaticals were also necessary to ensure continued involvement in scholarship. Brebner was sceptical about the use of "Ph. Deities" as the only measuring rods for *teachers* (p 48). Given the small size of the academic community, he thought there was "no compelling reason why Canadian college teachers need to be expected to hold any degree beyond a truly distinguished bachelor's one in the discipline which they pursue" (p 49), provided that the individual was well known and had at least two years of travel and study.

For those who elected to do graduate work he advised a rigorous weeding-out process. His hope was that in pursuit of the PH.D. "the specialization which it properly demands should be made to serve, not allowed to eclipse, broad intellectual cultivation." For Brebner, "two accompaniments of the transformations wrought by industrialization, laissez-faire philosophy and the division of labour, have had devastating effects on scholarship" (p 60).

While hard in his demands for proper teaching, Brebner had no doubt that professors should govern universities. He wrote:

> No university should be "run" by its president and deans, for the life-blood of scholarship flows upward from scholars, not downward from administrators who can seldom find time to keep up with a single scholarly discipline, let alone several, and who ordinarily do not have much contact with advanced students. For the health of scholarship deans ought to be kept thoroughly uneasy by

rigorously-maintained pushing and pulling between lively faculties and intelligent, consistent university policies.
(p 40)

Brebner's suggestions for improving scholarship in Canada were
often pointed and practical—ample funding for graduate studies
and research, a truly national library, and endorsement of the
value of scholarship. His suggestions in this respect did not rest
upon the will of the highest scholarly bodies such as the Royal Society, whose "meetings have been rather drowsy gatherings of
pleasant urbanity, but little distinction" (p 65). Rather he toyed
with the notion that Canada *needed* its own cadre of scholars.

Later, in a convocation address at McMaster University on 26
October 1945, Brebner amplified some of the points contained in
his report. He argued that "mankind has never been able to stand
still" (p 16) and so for all cultures the advancement of higher education was essential. General education and research was "the
communication of our living tradition and the quest of remedies for
its inadequacies" (p 2). While most students would not become
scholars, at the same time their education would form the basis of
their culture and citizenship and "in their proper modesty they
would know better than to become Philistines" (p 4). For those
with the special gift of original thinking, training in research must
be provided in order for them to help society advance. Brebner was
conscious of the test of social utility used in measuring the worth of
university activity and hoped that the public would support the loftier purposes of advanced studies. As he stated:

Canadians have hitherto focused their ambitions on such
narrow and short-sighted utilitarianism, and have been so

disdainful of the so-called impractical that their culture
has been almost entirely a feeble derivative from Great
Britain and the United States, and a large proportion of the
most fertile-minded young Canadians has quite naturally
left Canada in order to cross the Atlantic or the international boundary and work in more appreciative, cultivated,
congenial, and stimulating surroundings. (pp 19–20)

For Brebner the brain drain and the infusion of large numbers of
foreign academics or foreign training were symptomatic of a failure
of national purpose. As he concluded, "I believe that Canada
today is mature enough, intelligent enough, and rich enough to
chart her own intellectual course. Canada need not be resigned to
making over second-hand intellectual garments" (p 23).

Reactions to *Scholarship for Canada* were varied. Most readers
were sympathetic to its call for national commitment to scholarship, though the thrust of some comments was that Canada should
continue to follow rather than to lead.[64] A number of academics, of
course, reacted against small points, particularly criticism of the
Royal Society. Perhaps the most amusing observations came from
historian James J. Talman of Western in his 6 June 1945 letter to
Brebner: "I agree that the position of the scholar in Canada is
deplorable, but there are some consolations. . . . I do not want
much more money for myself and God knows my salary is low
enough. There is still a lot of fun in reading and writing and not
having to conform."

Brebner again got into some newspaper controversies as a by-
product of his role as commentator on Canadian higher education.
In 1950 the *Toronto Star* printed an article allegedly based on an
interview with Brebner, which stated that salaries at the University

of Toronto were too low and that everything said about Canadian universities in *Scholarship in Canada*, written five years earlier, was still true. Brebner wrote a stern letter to the editor denying that the statements were made, but the article nevertheless created problems with the U of T administration.[65] Ironically, the low salary offered as well as a heavy workload had been detriments to Toronto's 1929 offer to hire back Brebner.[66]

Brebner, for his part, had always tried to encourage Canadian scholarship. In 1940 he wrote to the Canadian millionaire, Sir Harry Oakes, shortly before the latter's murder, urging that he endow a chair of Canadian Affairs at a great American university. In 1954 there was a project to establish a centre for North Atlantic Studies in Canada, which also involved the Toronto history department and Frank Scott of McGill. At the time of *Scholarship in Canada* Brebner also confided in a letter to E.K. Brown of the University of Chicago English department, that "Innis has already done a good deal by way of exchange professorships, and I know he plans to promote the idea in other fields, but as you say, once one gets away from Canadian topics the sense of isolation is great."[67]

The controversy that surrounded Brebner in the last years of his life was inappropriate for a person who did not adhere in a formal way to any set philosophy. The charge of "Pinko" was absurd, for he was the least inclined to Communism. Once, while criticizing John Strachey and others for the belief that the sequence of events in recent history must lead to the triumph of Communism, he stated:

My confidence in history, therefore, is unlike that of the man who, when asked whether he believed in baptism, said that of course he did, he'd seen it. I think of history as

a method of useful but imperfect diagnosis of the present
by assessing the interplay of tradition in its various forms
with continuing change in its equally varied ones. It cannot
cope with chance. No historian is entitled to say that any
course of events was or is inevitable.[68]

Brebner's former students recall little conscious articulation
by him of a philosophy of history. R.K. Webb remembers that
Brebner recommended Keith Hancock's autobiography. There
Hancock described how partisan he could become while engross-
ing himself in documents, a partisanship that was constantly fluc-
tuating.[69] Ultimately the various contemporary views would
coalesce in the historian's view as he withdrew from the subject-
matter. This seemed to be Brebner's way too after exploration of
the minds of the historical figures he surveyed.

The fact that dozens of historians should go over his works on
Nova Scotia in fine detail, working up criticisms in the process,
undoubtedly would not have disturbed Brebner, for the search for
truth was constant. As he said of the Carnegie volumes, students
in twenty-five years would learn as much about how the climate of
opinion influenced authors' use of information as about the historical questions themselves.[70] Brebner, as his 1954 Columbia University address revealed, believed that "humility was man's best common ground."

CHAPTER SIX

AN INTERVIEW WITH GERALD S. GRAHAM

Gerald Graham (1903–88), like his friend Bartlet Brebner, earned much of his fame while teaching abroad. As Rhodes Professor of Imperial History at the University of London from 1949 to 1970, he trained some 200 academics now spread throughout the Commonwealth. But he never broke his ties with Canada. As Glyn Williams has said, the Canadian university posts held by his former students stretch out like stops on the Trans-Canada Highway. Graham also returned briefly to teach again in Canada after his retirement from the Rhodes chair in 1970.

There were also other ways in which his homeland continued to be important to him. Though his many books embraced the broad historical sweep of Britain's far-flung empire in the Atlantic, Indian, and Pacific oceans, Graham also dealt with Canada within this context. Historians of Canada were often guests at his imperial history seminar and he likewise made frequent appearances at

Canadian schools, exchanging views with Donald Creighton and
other noted Canadianists. He also had a lifelong keen interest in
Canadian public affairs.

Graham's career is an interesting one embracing teaching experiences in three countries and encounters with well-known figures
around the world. His wit and honesty also lend a vivid personal
perspective to the historical and public issues discussed in the following interview. Young historians and members of other profes-
sions will also enjoy and be encouraged by his frank description of
the twists and turns encountered in his lengthy career. To quote
Ian Steele, who presented him for conferral of an honorary LL.D.
from the University of Western Ontario two years before his death,
Gerald Graham is a "distinguished Canadian of global reputation."*

*The following interview took place in Charlottetown, PEI, on 12 Oc-
tober 1985. Some portions used elsewhere in this book are not included and a few items were added, deleted, and rearranged with
Professor Graham's consent.

I will just try to get some of your early background here.
My father was a Presbyterian minister and came out from Britain
as a young clergyman. He met my mother, at, of all places, a
Moody-Sankey conference in Chicago. They were married and
lived in the States—he went to Westminster College at Princeton,
New Jersey. Eventually they moved to Canada, to Sudbury,
Ontario, where I was born. They left Sudbury when I was four,
transferring to Madoc in Hastings County, a village which, in
memory, I still cherish. So I had a very happy boyhood—seven

years in Madoc just up to the outbreak of the 14—18 war. And then
from there we moved to Markham. The town has in the recent past
been hopelessly ravished by Toronto. I understand it's now the
wealthiest small town in Canada—it was a neat little village in my
day and I hate to think of what has happened to it. But from there I
went to Queen's and the family moved down to Puce, a little ham-
let on Lake St. Clair near Windsor.

**Was history your major subject of interest at Queen's as an un-
dergraduate?**
Yes. It was so in high school. I almost went to Toronto; we were
living close by to Toronto, but I only had a bare pass in mathematics. Queen's would let me in, and Toronto wouldn't. So I went
to Queen's. My life at Queen's was happy. I have studied at various universities, four or five of them, but the Queen's existence
was exceptionally pleasant, and there were some outstanding men
there at the time. In history, I fell under the influence of J.L. Morrison, a product of Glasgow University. I know youngsters are supposed to be under somebody's influence. I think discipleship can
be carried too far; I don't believe in devout disciples anyway. But I
will say that Morrison, though he may at times have gone in for
histrionics, was the perfect teacher for the undergraduate. He
lifted you to the skies and occasionally you were dropped. But I
never will forget his lectures and I copied them out in better handwriting from the scrambled original. As a callow bumpkin from the
country I headed his class in colonial history, I think it was called,
at Christmas time. We became friends and kept in touch until his
death. He left, most tragically for me, the next year, and his place
was taken by Duncan MacArthur, who was the absolute opposite in
personality. He later became a good friend of mine but his whole

personality lacked the excitement of Morrison and it took me a couple of years to get used to MacArthur and to appreciate his professional approach to history through documents, however.

You were exposed to Morrison in your first year?
Yes, I was interested and intended to major in history anyway. Morrison, without exaggeration, lifted me up. Looking backwards you could see that he overcoloured, but undergraduate teaching is important, and he offered a marvelous sketch of the growth of empire. When he left for England to take the chair at Armstrong College, later called the University of Newcastle (he left largely because of his wife's health), I just felt bereft.

Was W.L. Grant another of your mentors?
Yes. He became a great friend of mine. This is how we met. I came back to do my MA at Queen's, though chiefly to edit the *Queen's Journal*, which I missed out on the year before. I took my MA and a year later they gave me the Queen's Fellowship to go to Harvard. The Harvard connections, which were developed later when I went to teach there, were slim at the time. I disliked the graduate school of Harvard intensely. I was back to writing essays and routine tasks that I rebelled against. The Queen's acting principal, W.E. MacNeil, who was a great friend of mine, was then Registrar, and recommended me to W.L. Grant for a Sir George Parkin Fellowship tenable in England. At that time, I hadn't yet gone to Harvard; this was the year before. I met Grant and applied for the Parkin Scholarship. I was selling real estate at the time in Detroit. Previously I had various summer jobs while at Queen's—lumber mills, waiter on the Great Lakes boats, machine shop at Ford's, and then I ended up selling real estate. This last was preceded by

a cattle-boat trip to England, which was for me a thrilling adventure.

As a youngster I had been brought up on British fiction, including *Chums* and *The Boys' Own Paper*. After all, my parents came from the Old Country. But my attachments were not especially imperial, as I think I have said in a little book I wrote, *Tides of Empire*. There was nothing jingoistic in my attitude. I remember in 1910 singing in school when George V was crowned and how every "savage chieftain" was expected to bow and honour him. All this was part of my upbringing, the Empire and the love of Britain. The cattle-boat, (ss *Turcoman*) that brought me to Avonmouth (the port of Bristol) after a trip of two weeks, really was the climax of dreams. I walked around Bristol all that night with Professor J. A. Roy, from the Queen's English department, who was on the cattle-boat with us. Thence to London and eventually to stay with an aunt and uncle in Harpenden. But I had introductions to Sir Edward Peacock, a Queen's man, and senior partner in Baring Brothers and Director of the Bank of England, including directorships with the CPR and the Hudson Bay Company; and to Lord Beaverbrook; and I met Dawson of *The Times*.

Meanwhile J. L. Morrison had asked me to visit him in Newcastle, as did an uncle in Edinburgh. So after a cycle trip, which took me as far as Naples and Venice, I took the train for Newcastle, the Roman Wall, and Edinburgh. Meanwhile in Edinburgh a letter came from *The Times* saying that my application for a job had been favourably considered and I was offered a post of sub-editor in the foreign news department. It was a frightening invitation for one whose experience was limited to editing the *Queen's Journal*. However, I might add that there are all sorts of sub-editors. Beaverbrook's editor-in-chief, Blumenfeld, had turned me down, which is probably just as well. He probably thought I didn't look the aggressive type that would suit the *Express*. And he was quite right, I would have been scared stiff at the thought of following the adventures of some of my more experienced journalist friends or acquaintances. However, *The Times*, more sedate, had many attractions, but I was on my way to Edinburgh, and the job was in London. Should I go back? I decided not to. So I declined *The Times* offer.

Later on, reading last year an autobiographical sketch by the novelist, Graham Greene, it seems that in August of the same year he was appointed sub-editor in the foreign news department of *The Times*. It would appear that he got my job; otherwise I can only think we could have been mates in the same business. But it is interesting to ponder what might have happened had I accepted. The experience might have toughened me. So I went back to Canada, and at the end of the summer of 1925 I got a job in Detroit as labourman with a building firm (my MA didn't count) and from there I went into Allan Gardens Real Estate.

It was at this time that I wrote to W.L. Grant applying for the Parkin Scholarship to England. Vincent Massey was on the selection board, and he apparently didn't like the idea of anybody applying on such flamboyant notepaper, topped by the slogan: "Buy Allan Gardens." It was, nevertheless, a good strong paper. Grant wrote back and he said, "As a fellow Queen's man, I regret that you lost out to one who was judged to have a lead over you" (it turned out to be a clergyman). And he added: "for heaven's sake next time use decent notepaper; ambassadors are kittle-cattle, Vincent Massey didn't like your Allan Gardens notepaper"! So the following year (when I went to Harvard on the Queen's Fellowship), I bought the most expensive bond paper you can imagine

and applied again. At Christmas time, 1926, I was entertained at
dinner by the Grants in the Principal's residence at Upper Canada
College, and later on, to my great joy, learned that my second bid
was successful. I went to Cambridge University because I saw a
note in the *Queen's Journal* that they were offering an exhibition at
Trinity College open to citizens of the Empire. I think it was still
called the Empire (wouldn't it have been in 1927?). Anyway, the
encouragement of imperial or Commonwealth studies was the aim,
and this was for me an extra £40 a year. So I applied and got it.
Later on thanks to my tutor at Trinity it was raised to £100, plus
my athletic fees.

Grant never sent my money on time and I used to borrow from
the great man (whose life I started to write, but eventually passed it
on to Donald Schurman), Sir Edward R. Peacock. It was through
this Parkin Scholarship that I got to know Peacock, who thought I
was the worst financier he had ever met. I always remember when,
short of cash, I went to Baring Brothers, 8 Bishopsgate. Peacock
would ring a bell and one of the clerks would walk in with, say,
£50, piled on a silver tray. I was so overcome I didn't even offer
him a receipt. But he always got his money back.

Peacock was a Canadian?
Oh yes. Peacock was from Glengarry County. I became, I suppose,
his literary executor for such of his private papers that were left after his unfortunate bonfires. Most were destroyed, especially those
dealing with the royal family, for whom he was financial adviser.
They are now in the hands of Queen's. His is a fascinating story of
teaching at Upper Canada College; thence to Dominion Securities,
Toronto, and then from Dominion Securities to London where he
had connections with that famous Bank of England man, Montague

Norman, and then he went on to the top. The Bank unveiled a plaque to his memory, two or three years ago, in a ceremony which I attended. It is a life that I think should be written. I had weekly interviews with Peacock over two years before his death.

Grant also taught at Upper Canada?
Probably, but I am not certain, but he did marry a daughter of the then Principal, Sir George Parkin. He returned to Upper Canada as Principal after leaving the History Department at Queen's. Grant and Peacock would be about the same age. I think Peacock was about ninety-one when he died, or ninety-two.

Now when you went to Cambridge, who was your mentor?
My tutor was an American called Gaillard Lapsley, a friend of Henry James and Edith Wharton, who became more English than the English; my supervisor was John Holland Rose. Harold Innis once said, "I can see [in something I had written] the hand of Holland Rose in this." I wrote back and said no. Holland Rose's influence in the naval field was nil; what he did give me was abiding friendship and some self-confidence. We became good friends, and I would maintain that, at a certain stage of life, giving a pupil self-confidence is even more important than scholarly techniques. He was old for a university teacher; I think he was heading towards seventy then. He didn't know much about my subject, which concerned eighteenth-century trade policy, but I had freedom to pursue my searches everywhere. As was the custom, I visited him once a week, and read him something I had written. But I wanted to meet, and squeeze nourishment from all available sources. Many names were known to me from undergraduate days at

Queen's. Soon I met Trevelyan, Temperley, Ernest Barker, and, in London, G.P. Gooch and Lillian Penson.[2] I used to read thesis chapters to Trevelyan. I remember particularly reading him something I had written on the Quebec Act, demolishing, so I boldly assumed, Reginald Coupland, who was the Beit Professor at Oxford. Later on, Trevelyan arranged that I address the Cambridge Historical Society, which included senior staff as well as graduate students, on the subject of the Quebec Act.

Then you did your PH.D. Some Canadians in the past found the Cambridge system hard to take in the sense that they found it very loose, the fact that so much depends on personal initiative.
That's what I liked about it. After Harvard the freedom was wonderful. I have just been reading Volume I of Lord Clarke's autobiography: *A Life of Kenneth Clarke*. He went to Oxford for his undergraduate studies, and rarely attended any lectures. But he did manage successfully to live a nourishing life of his own. I went to as many lectures as I could manage, even those of my tutor, Gaillard Lapsley, on medieval history, though I doubt if I got much out of them. But the freedom I cherished. One got away from this dispiriting routine business of weekly or bi-weekly essays and sessional exams and so on. I suppose most techniques such as you acquire are passed on to you by the people you associate with. I used to spend all my vacations in the public archives in Chancery Lane, apart from Christmas time, when I played hockey for Cambridge. We toured Europe; that was another fruitful experience.

Hockey was played more in those days in Britain I guess?
It was just beginning to open up on the continent. At Queen's I was

on the Arts Faculty team. I wouldn't have made the first team. As it happened I learned more about hockey in Europe than I ever did at Queen's because I was playing all the time during the tours. And we played in Belgium, Germany (Hitler's Sports Palace in Berlin), and the final game against Oxford in Switzerland. And you stayed in the best hotels; this was a luxurious life I wasn't accustomed to.

Getting back to the PH.D., what was your thesis topic?

I nearly lost out on that. It was called "British Policy and Canada, 1774–1791" and, through ignorance, I just called it "A Study in 18th Century Mercantilism." Oh! It was a fool thing to do; I had no political sense. Who should they put on my board but two economists and one of them was the great Sir John Clapham and the other, thank God, had been in Toronto and had just moved over to Cambridge, as Reader in Economics, C.R. Fay. He had been a professor in the University of Toronto for about ten years. He, I believe, saved my life. When the interview began, Clapham said, "What do you know about mercantilism?" He said, "it's the study of money and your book is not a study of money." When the examination was over it was clear that Clapham wasn't sure whether I had covered new ground or made any new discoveries. Fay came to my rescue and was positive in my defence. In the end, a settlement must have been reached, for the thesis was passed and was subsequently published in the Imperial Studies series under the editorship of the Rhodes Professor of Imperial History, A.P. Newton. The revised subtitle read: *A Study in 18th Century Trade Policy*. When I told the story very briefly at my eightieth birthday celebration in London, I remarked that I would undoubtedly have failed had I not, at the end of the examination, slipped Sir John Clapham a £5 note, thus making sure of my PH.D. I don't know how many of the audience believed me!

When you finished at Cambridge your first job was at Harvard?
Yes. Thanks to my tutor and his friendship with a dynamic professor in the History Department, Roger Merriman, I was approached by Harvard. Again, note that embossed paper comes into the business. For the second time I was using borrowed notepaper in my application, nicely adorned and labelled Cambridge Students Union. The answering letter came back to the Union headquarters, and sat in a pigeonhole for two or three weeks. I had been offered the job, but in the meantime had been awarded an English Rockefeller Fellowship to study colonial history in Europe. Finding myself caught in this painful dilemma, I panicked, and rushed off for help from my tutor Gaillard Lapsley, an austere bachelor who lived in Neville's Court. It was eight o'clock in the morning, far outside visiting hours, when I stood in front of his door, for the moment too petrified to knock. Suddenly the door opened and there he stood in his underwear, retrieving his bottle of milk. I was told some time later by Kitson Clark, a Trinity don, that I was undoubtedly the first person in England ever to see Lapsley in his underwear, and that was enough to damn any man for life! When I was finally admitted at ten, he said, "Graham, I don't know what your case is but you probably ruined it already." And then in the end he sat down and said, "I'll send a cable to Merriman explaining the situation and seeing if the appointment can be postponed, but you, Graham, will pay for the cablegram." So he got me out of it and I went to Germany. I went first to Berlin, where I played hockey for the Ger-

mans, as well as working on German colonial policy. Then, after a skiing holiday in Austria, to Freiburg-im-Breisgau where I met that fine scholar, Gerhard Ritter.[3] And it was to Ritter, some years later, that I sent Bob Spencer before he went to Toronto.[4]

This would have been in the early 1930s?
I got my PH.D. in 1929, thence to Germany '29–'30. Meanwhile, Queen's further complicated my existence. I remember sitting in Florence towards the end of my Rockefeller year wondering if Queen's would answer my letter because there had been tentative suggestions by Professor MacArthur that I go back to Queen's. MacArthur delayed writing. Back in England, and still no news from Queen's, Harvard repeated their offer, and I accepted. Meanwhile, before I got back to Canada, a couple of months later, MacArthur learned of this from me, and wrote to Harvard saying, Graham has no future at Harvard; "it is a highly competitive place and we want him at Queen's." Arthur Schlesinger, Sr. wrote back (he was chairman of the department then), and said, "we will let him make up his own mind, we might like to keep him here; you never can tell," or words to that effect. And so, back in Kingston it was agreed in conversation with MacArthur, I should go to Harvard for a year and then return to Queen's.

Well, I was tempted by the devil, because at the end of the year at Harvard, they offered me the first lectureship in Canadian history that had been given as a straight course, as well as a course in modern English history at Radcliffe, the women's college which was associated with Harvard. This brought my salary from $2,000. to $3,500. The Queen's offer remained, I suppose at $2,200. I was tempted to stay, but the main impulse was not the devil of greed.

Harvard had a great history school in those days. Nonetheless, in retrospect, I do believe that under the encroaching shadow of the Depression, the authorities should have been a little more cautious in their advice. Anyhow such doubts as may have possessed me were conquered. Harvard seemed the place for me. The future was rosy. I recall W.S. Ferguson, the Canadian from PEI, eminent in Greek history, saying, "There are many of the professorial staff getting $8,000; there is no reason why you shouldn't." Indeed, three or four, including Ferguson himself, were getting $12,000. Anyhow, I took the gamble, and burned my boats to Queen's; and for the next five years made lasting friendships, particularly with Bill Langer and Fred Merk, and eventually with Roger Merriman, to whose collegiate residence, Eliot House, I became attached.[5]

But soon the Depression began to bite. I had been given a three-year appointment, which used to mean stability, on the edge of tenure. But when time ran out the president began to dispose of a whole younger generation of staff under the rank of associate professor. By themselves, they could have formed a complete and good university, according to the dean, whose conversation partook of an apology. (I think his name was Burbank, an economist.) Everyone in my history group went but one, Paul Buck, who later became provost. Well! There were very few jobs to be found; the unemployed, potential instructors and professors, sat in groups on the steps of the Widener Library, a desolate scene. The Depression really hit academia in the U.S. When I went back to Queen's, there was little or no sign of it. Even, shall I say, the B class seemed secure in their jobs, or so it appeared, in the light of my American experience. In brief, President Conant had abolished the tutorial system started by Lowell when he was president. It was

simply disbanded. Meanwhile, Queen's remained in ignorance of
my fate. Reginald Trotter was now head of the department, and apparently regarded me as one of their successful (I'm trying to think
of a not immodest title) graduates, one that had made good outside
the bounds of Canada, and was therefore deserving of attention.
Trotter wrote me and said that "we need an addition to the department. We're growing. Can you recommend a young man to come
here and join the History Department at $1,800 a year?" I showed
the letter to Merk, Merk wrote to Trotter. I got the job. I went back
to Queen's, $1,800 a year with my family (having previously been
paid $3,500), and very glad to have a job and particularly in my
old University for which I had a great affection.

**Do you think if the Depression hadn't hit Harvard so hard, you
would have been happy to stay on there and perhaps in time become an American citizen?**
It is possible. I mean, Merk and Langer, particularly Merk, used
to say in a kindly way (I wouldn't take it too seriously), that Harvard were damn fools to get rid of me. That's a bit of nonsense, because they cleared out the whole group. But that's not an answer to
your question. I think at the time, I remember talking to Professor
C.H. McIlwain, reminding him that in Cambridge and Oxford
there were places for tutors who didn't even write very much. And
under the tutorial system, as Lowell founded it, there was a large
group who were primarily concerned with teaching. McIlwain
replied that sadly there was no longer room for that system at Harvard. Yes, I felt I could have been happy there; certainly New England was attractive and Boston, in those days, was a lovely town.
And I had good friends there. I have already mentioned Merk and
Langer, who were particularly close, and Merriman. We're all vic-

tims of chance and who was it, Lord Haldane, I think, who said he would hate to live his life over again for fear the same element of luck wouldn't enter into it. When I left Harvard I thought my career was finished; a disastrous blow had been suffered, so I thought. I couldn't see any light ahead and I was thirty-three. Then Queen's gave me a second start, and it was sheer joy to be back in Kingston. It was starting all over again. And little did I think then that I would be doing the same thing once again when I went to England.

So through the remainder of the thirties you were at Queen's?

I went to Queen's in the autumn of '36. I stayed there until, I think the beginning of '41—how many years is that? That's about five years. I remember I was one year short for a sabbatical. Then the war came.

Did you teach British history?

I taught all things, I taught American history largely based on an old Harvard student's notes. When Harrison, who had been teaching English history, went away to Oxford, to try to get a higher degree, I taught English history. Trotter did the colonial, occasionally I helped out, and I ran a seminar in Canadian history which James Conacher, Stuart Webster, Fred Gibson, and Malcolm Mac-Donell attended, along with four or five others. I was very happy there and they made me an assistant professor a year later, and then I got the Guggenheim Fellowship. The next morning following the announcement, I found, facing me on the seminar table, a bottle of rum and a plaque draped in the Queen's colours containing a poetic inscription with the pictures and signatures of the whole class. I still treasure it.

A Guggenheim Fellowship meant going back to the U.S. I went
first to Columbia, where Brebner fixed me up with accommodation
and introductions. I was then writing a book, which became
*Empire of the North Atlantic. Sea Power and British North Amer-
ica, 1783–1820* had already been published by Harvard University Press. I had no wish to stay in New York for a year, and I
thought of Florida and sunshine. So I went to the executive boss of
the Guggenheim Trust, Henry Moe, and to my surprise he was de-
lighted with the idea and said, "you are the first man in the history
of this Fellowship who suggested he would like to spend a large
part of his time in a holiday resort, and I am all for it." Thanks to
an old friend of my father's, we got a cottage on a lovely beach at
Sarasota on the Gulf of Mexico. And the Sarasota Library arranged
to have photostats of British Admiralty correspondence sent down
from the Library of Congress, a tremendous boon. So I was able to
work away partly in the Library, in company with Richard Alding-
ton, who was writing his *Life of Wellington*, and partly in my comfortable office, our little garage, close to the beach. Apart from ex-
cursions, there was little to interrupt almost six months of
pleasurable toil on *Empire of the North Atlantic*.

Meanwhile, on the way back to Canada, I stopped at Harvard to
do a spot of work in the Widener. There were still two or three
months of the Guggenheim to spare. I was just getting settled in my
small Widener study when along came a telephone call from Commander Kenneth Ketchum, on leave as headmaster of St.
Andrews. He said the Canadian Navy chaps were organizing a
naval college at Royal Roads, close by Esquimalt, "and since you
are one man who knows some naval history, you have been recommended to us." I think Glazebrook had something to do with it.[6] In
any event, Ketchum came all the way down to Harvard to see if he

could get me. Once again, tempted by such ardent attentions, I said fine. Although already in the Queen's OTC, I accepted and was poured into naval uniform as Lieutenant Commander when I got to Montreal. It was agreed, however, that I should be allowed time at sea, and hopefully the chance to visit the UK every summer, assuming transport was available. Fine, fine. So I was flown to England, which I had become entranced with following my cattle-boat trip in 1925.

So that is why at the beginning of the war you wanted to have this arrangement that you would visit Britain at least once a year?
Oh yes, I wanted to get back to England; I didn't want to be cloistered on the west coast for the duration. From then on they allowed me to gain my limited nautical experience on British destroyers and on one American "4-stacker" doing convoy duty. My old friend A.R.M. Lower (who saw naval service in the First World War) said to me recently, "Oh I suppose you just sat at a desk all during the war did you?" (By the way, he really is a good friend of mine, although I once made bold to tell him how I felt particularly sceptical about his advocacy of an artificial nationalism.) "That's not quite right," I said. "I crossed the ocean four times in destroyers." "That's all right, that's all right," he said. When I was working on *Empire of the North Atlantic,* he had written to me that I should practise landing on the beach even in a rowboat just to get the smell of salt—"row, row and row ashore pretending." This was shortly before the U.S. entered the war.

Were you involved with any Canadian historians, during the war, who were working on the official history?
Yes. I didn't even mention it in *Who's Who* because I didn't do a

good job. At the end of the war HQ were going to bring me back to
Canada. I said I wanted to write the history of the Canadian Navy
and they wouldn't touch me at the time. Rather than go back to
Canada and through the influence of my friend Kenneth Stuart,
who was a lieutenant general, they got me transferred from the
navy to the historical section of the army. This was towards the end
of 1944. And my reason for switching was perfectly selfish, I
didn't want to leave England and go back and sit peacefully on the
west coast. A few months later, naval HQ must have had a change
of heart because they asked me if I would come back to the navy. I
felt it would not be decent to reverse again. So I stayed in the historical section of the army until the end of the war. It was then that
I was offered a job in the history department at Edinburgh and appear to have accepted it. I didn't realize having been interviewed
that they had appointed me without mentioning it at the time. I
thought they would offer me a written notice. I had serious doubts,
on further consideration, and I took the night train to Edinburgh,
apologized and resigned. Then it looked as if I would be going
back to Queen's because Queen's had made me an associate professor in my absence and a full professor if I came back, at something like $4,500—which was a lot of money. Edinburgh, I think,
was £800. Once again, I faced an awful dilemma. Is this the second or the third time I start over again? I forget. Anyway, with
Edinburgh I had closed the door. J.L. Morrison did his best for me;
he was still alive and he told them they ought to offer me a readership, not a lectureship. Eventually after a few sleepless nights I
accepted a lectureship at Birkbeck College, London, at £550 a
year. That meant turning down Queen's. This business of starting
life over again from the bottom was getting a bit much. It was

a gamble. You can never be sure when a gamble will pay off. The same year Birkbeck raised my salary to £660.

What was the major consideration in your decision to go with Birkbeck. Was it the idea of staying on in England, that you wanted to be there?
I think we left out a primary consideration—marriage to that person you have just seen entering the kitchen. I shall lock the door on her to teach her she should remain in the kitchen. Joking aside, I have no doubt that the fact that she was in England had an important bearing; otherwise it is difficult to think of somebody taking £550 and giving up Queen's, and I remained devoted to Queen's.

Did you think that this might mean that the rest of your academic career would be in Britain? It was a conscious decision?
Oh yes. All my life I had the feeling that I would like to live in England partly because it is close to the Continent—not just England itself. When we take a holiday we go to the Continent; we go to Italy or we go to France or, now in our old age, I'll soon be eighty-four, we go to the Canary Islands. And last spring we went to Tunisia. But these things, I don't think, can be easily explained. I've often said it is not where you are born, it is what you are born. I've known Scots and Germans who have made fine North Americans, just suited them to a T. Take my wife's family, migrating from England and Scotland and making good, perfect Canadians. Then you get the reverse. Some Canadians going the other way.

Yes. It always seems unnatural. Like Americans residing in Europe.
When I was giving the Wiles lectures in Belfast in 1963, (they

were subsequently published as a book, *The Politics of Naval Strategy*), Preston of RMC chided me gently for being an expatriate.

Was this Richard Preston?
Yes. He's an expatriate himself now, Duke University, North Carolina. But I remember him saying that I was talking as an expatriate. There is a feeling among some Canadians that you have the right to move one way, but to move the other way is unnatural.

Luck, as I say, plays a part. You can't overdo that business of luck. As in the army, if the right man is killed the next man becomes colonel. Reginald Coupland had a row with his Oxford bosses and in a huff resigned from the Beit Chair of Colonial History. The job went to Vincent Harlow, who was the Rhodes Professor of Imperial History, King's College, London. His translation left a vacancy and I applied. After a nerve-racking interview (they had delegates from Cambridge and Oxford on the selection board), they offered me the chair. I might have missed it for one silly reason. Admiral Thursfield, a great friend of mine (to whom I dedicated one of my books), wanted me to meet the principal of King's College, Sir William Halliday, who he said, was the boss—"he's the one who really fixes these things, and you must meet him. Join me for lunch at the Athenaeum." (I wasn't a member then.) Thursfield could not locate the principal and suggested we go down to the billards room; the principal normally played billiards after lunch. Unhappily he shoved me through the door just as the principal was about to make a stroke, and I jarred his moving arm. Whether the ball went into the pocket I very much doubt. Anyhow I thought, "there goes my chance for the Rhodes Chair." Of all the damnfool introductions that have ever been made, this one, to the principal of King's, topped the bill! I reminded him of this later. He was an austere man; you did not banter lightly with him. But on this occasion he roared with laughter. Anyway I got the appointment.

Had all the holders of the Rhodes Chair until that time been British?
Well, yes. There have not been many. The man who really was the first professor was the famous A.P. Newton, who had been a chemist and turned historian. The man before him had been a lecturer; the Chair itself was held first by Newton. I tried to get a Readership established later, when I became a friend of Beaverbrook, I won't say a client, but a friend who tipped me bits of information every now and then, such as a conversation of President Roosevelt, when he didn't know that Beaverbrook was listening next door, to the effect that he hoped that the United States would get Newfoundland for keeps. I have that in Beaverbrook's handwriting. This was a kind of repayment for minor help on his educational committee that provided scholarships for Maritimers. I tried to launch a scheme for a Beaverbrook Readership in imperial history. He'd supply the money and thus establish his immortality. Twice Beaverbrook phoned me in reply to my queries and each time I was out. And his secretary, Miller, said after the first time, "Beaverbrook never tries twice." When he did try a second time to get me and I was out (I was in Cambridge) Miller said, "you are finished; he will never try again." And he didn't. But he did ask my wife and myself down for lunch at his country house, along with the Duke and Duchess of Argyll. We had a great lunch. But when you're being offered hospitality and treated most royally, you can't say: "Look, I have a scheme whereby you can invest a couple of hundred thousand and win immortality." I didn't do it and the sub-

ject never arose again. But I have often thought that if I had struck
Beaverbrook at the right time he would have provided a Readership in imperial history in his name. This I say in passing.

What was your rank just before you got the Rhodes professorship?
I had been made a Reader at the end of my second year at Birkbeck College.

So it was only within a year or two of that, was it?
Oh, yes. In 1947 I was a lecturer, in 1948 I became a Reader, and
I left for the Chair in January 1949. So I was Reader just for part of
a year.

So this is a rapid rise in British academic life?
It depends on where the openings are. It would be a rapid rise if
you were in one place. But I moved location, from Birkbeck by the
Senate House to Kings' College on the Strand. The Chair was
tenable at King's.

**To what extent did your occupation of the Rhodes Chair widen the
field of your interests and researches? Hitherto, the North Atlantic
seems to have been your domain.**
My new job at King's College was almost entirely responsible for
the widening of my horizons. Some time in the early fifties a
shrewd pundit remarked that the post-war Commonwealth was a
loose association of nations held together by the BA and B.SC. degrees from London University. Most of the new universities in Africa were founded under London's auspices.

In my first year at King's (1949) I gave a special lecture course
for Colonial Office cadets (future District Officers) who were being

rapidly enlisted to oversee the last days of empire, especially in Africa and Malaya. As a partial reward for such exertions, I was given a trip to the Gold Coast to attend a summer school conference in January 1951 at Cape Coast. I stayed at St. Augustine's College, a Catholic missionary base, where the brothers were uncommonly kind to me. My introduction to Africa was notable for two incidents. On my first night, following a "High Life" dance, I fell down a deep, concrete drainage channel, and a slight cut festered, as they have a habit of doing in the tropics, into a serious infection. I credit my eventual recovery to the administrations of a Nigerian witch doctor, but that happy feeling of complete resurrection did not come until I breathed the cool air at some twenty or so thousand feet in my homeward-bound airplane. My second eventful introduction occurred during an open-air conference, when I told an evening audience of some 1,000 mosquito-harassed students that they were getting their independence too soon. A low and ominous hum as from a large swarm of bees rapidly reached a crescendo, and my old student, Dennis Austin (who helped to organize the meeting), rushed out for help to prevent a lynching. However, I hastened to shout out above the rising clamour that my son John, at present stationed in Ottawa with the Department of External Affairs, would, I hoped, be the first Canadian ambassador to the new nation of Ghana. There was silence, then laughter, and finally loud applause. The atmosphere had changed within seconds. I was saved. Thenceforward, I visited the west coast almost every year during the spring vacation, where I acted as history examiner, chiefly at Ibadan in Nigeria. My first African London PH.D. student Kenneth Dike was to become the first African vice-chancellor of Ibadan. In fact, my West African graduate students were of unusual quality. Like Dike, Jacob Ajayi and Emmanuel Ayandele became distinguished historians and for a time they too served as vice-chancellors, at Lagos and Calabar respectively. Another task which was to take me to Sierra Leone and up the Gambia was the enlistment of authors for my West Africa history series, launched by Cecil King, the publisher of the *Daily Mirror*.

I spent one academic session at Makerere College, Uganda. I enjoyed college life (which was markedly British), but the chief excitements were a visit to the now near-ruinous national park, where my host and driver, Dr. Ray Beachey, with considerable daring took our frail car through hosts of nervous elephants and their offspring onto the river close to Murchism Falls with its countless exotic birds, hippos, and yawning crocodiles. Then at the end of term, a friendly chief justice arranged for me to join a police detachment, sent northeast into the Karamojing region to counter Turkana raiders from over the Kenya border. I recall the tiny hamlets surrounded by double rows of tough thorn bushes, with narrow entrances that compelled the invader to crawl through on his or her hands and knees. There were many burned-out villages; and my study wall is adorned with a memento of that expedition—a giraffe-hide shield and two long spears, relics of the battlefield.

You spoke earlier of widening horizons. Was the move from the North Atlantic to the Indian Ocean (as exemplified in your book, *Britain in the Indian Ocean*) an inevitable process following on your London appointment?
Not really. It was a matter of my own pleasure. I needed a change of sea air. I wanted to extend my interests into, for me, unknown fields. I was tempted ever eastward, and the archival documents as

well as the arranged lecture tours on British imperial subjects guided me almost involuntarily. Not until some years later after the Uganda journey did I visit South Africa, thanks to the influence of old seminar students plus the generosity of the South Africa Foundation. But rather sadly most of my contacts were confined to university colleagues in towns and cities. The Simonstown base was important to me, because *Britain in the Indian Ocean* was getting under way. Similarly, a visit to Zanzibar was a most rewarding experience. I stayed for a week as a guest of the Resident, and thanks to his intervention, invaluable documents (in those last days of the British Raj) were brought to my room; from my desk I looked out on the coastline and the colorful dhows of another age that sailed the Indian Ocean. Thence, to Aden, where once again, thanks to the generous intervention of the Colonial Office, I was put up in the governor's residence, and subsequently, only days before the retreat of Britain's imperial legion, viewed the surrounding fortifications and mountain walls from a helicopter.

I would assume that your lecture engagements as well as your researches took you to India, and even further eastward as your interests and tastes developed?

For some eight years, Australian and New Zealand graduate students had attended my seminar. I told the Carnegie representative, who was visiting the UK, that it was high time the procedure was reversed. He responded with grace and cash. A generous grant from the British Council permitted a lecture tour on the way—Ceylon, India, Pakistan, Malaya, and Sarawak. All this fitted in with my aim to see and absorb something of the ethos of the countries bordering the Indian Ocean. My engagements took me from Colombo to the University of Ceylon in Peradynia; thence to Trincomalee, the famous land-locked naval base, and on from Trichinopoli and Madras as far north in Pakistan as the old army base at Quetta. Unhappily, my visit in 1957 was marred by the recent Suez operation, and the British Council in Delhi was fearful that an imperial historian, lecturing on the British Empire, might inflame national passions. Fortunately, Pakistan representatives were not so alarmed. As it turned out, only in Delhi and one or two other places was the command obeyed, and I was able to talk freely without riotous interruption.

Returning from Colombo, I then headed for Singapore and Kuching in Sarawak, where my family enjoyed the hospitality of Rajah Brooke's forsaken estate, especially the swimming pool, surrounded by exotic orchids. Meanwhile, I pursued my lecture tour in Malaya, beginning in Singapore, and on to Kuala Lumpur and Penang, before rejoining my wife in Kuching, where my lecture on the evolution of the Commonwealth was to my surprise subsequently translated, for propaganda purposes, into Chinese and French.

It was the tail end of empire, and we continued to benefit from government hospitality. The Resident provided a motor launch, well stocked with whisky, gin, and accompaniments, and we were able to spend a week sailing luxuriantly up the Rajang River as far into the interior as Kapit, visiting and entertaining or being entertained in Dyak long-houses along the way. The whole episode had a dream-like quality, and I cannot forget (nor did Malcolm Macdonald, then High Commissioner for South East Asia) the beauty of the topless Dyak maidens. We moved by ship around the Borneo islands, stopping at Labuan, Brunei, and Sandakan on the Celebes Sea, before returning to Singapore, whose sand-laden archive corridors provided little sustenance.

After a tedious flight via Darwin and Sydney we made our Australian headquarters in the National University of Canberra, an arrangement supported by Sir Keith Hancock, an old friend whom I had first met in Florence in 1925. There I worked continuously on printed sources, Dutch as well as English, with occasional bouts of lecturing in Sydney, Brisbane, Melbourne, and the University of Tasmania. Late in June 1958, we flew to Auckland, whence a pilgrimage of lectures took us to Wellington and Dunedin, in all of which it was a joy to meet old students. After that followed a flight to Fiji where I talked to both Indian and Fijian audiences, concluding with a lecture in Stanford, California, arranged by the Chancellor, Wallace Spirling, whom I had known in far-gone Canadian days. We, the six of us (wife, three children, and a nanny), had survived a hectic year around the world in 350 days! The three children were all under six, and they flourished.

What about Europe? Did your work or interests take you often across the Channel?
As it happened, shortly before war broke out, an article I had written for a Polish academic journal led to an invitation to visit Gdynia, Warsaw, and Cracow, where I met members of a great history school now helpless, if not destroyed, in the holocaust that followed. It was a sad journey; the general optimism worried me deeply at the time. It was the spring of 1939. The square miles of border lands with Germany were flat, an open invitation to Nazi tanks, and neither French nor British bombers could bridge the gap, and bring the help that a brave but ill-informed people expected. From Cracow I flew to Hungary; thence by train through the Balkans; to Istanbul by ship, then after a week, on to Athens, and north through a corner of Yugoslavia for a despairing farewell

visit to Munich. This was in August 1939. I returned to Germany in 1949. British and German academics had founded *Die Brucke* to "bridge" the long Nazi silence, to bring the released German victims, especially the intellectuals, once again in touch with the outside world. In successive years, I lectured on the old British Empire in Hamburg, Berlin, Heidelberg, Münster, and in Freiburg-im-Breisgau, where I was welcomed by my old teacher, Gerhard Ritter, saved from execution at the last moment by the arrival of Russian troops in Berlin.

Did you manage to keep up your Canadian connections during your years in the UK?
Very much so, and with the U.S. as well. We usually managed a visit every two or three years, especially to Toronto, my wife's birthplace, where the history department of the University of Toronto were exceedingly warm and welcoming. In 1967, I lectured in St. John's, Newfoundland, on the anniversary of Confederation. Later in the same year through the solicitation of old students, my wife and I pursued our leisurely way to Halifax, Fredericton, Quebec City, Kingston, London, Ontario, and away westward as far as Edmonton, where our hosts the two doughty Thomas's, Louis G. and Louis H., took us for a grand winter tour through the Rockies. Two years later, I gave three Reid lectures at Acadia University, which were subsequently published as *Tides of Empire*. As for my American contacts, back in 1951, I lectured in Columbia, New York, where an old and much-loved friend, J.B. Brebner, was still teaching. Thence to Princeton, New Jersey, to the Institute for Advanced Studies, where, for a half-year free of all duties, including lecturing (apart from a Cathedral address on the death of George VI), I was able to make a start on *Britain in the*

Indian Ocean. Eight years later we spent an enjoyable and fruitful half-year at the University of Wisconsin, in Madison. At long last I was to meet that sturdy protagonist of British Empire studies, Paul Knaplund. In 1970, I retired from London and accepted an invitation to lecture on the empire and seapower at the University of Western Ontario. There followed two good and indeed, energizing years, capped astonishingly enough, by an honorary degree in 1986.

There is a lot of correspondence in the archival files at Queen's between you and Innis.
Some of it is contained in Creighton's biography. I gave the letters to Creighton before he wrote the book. You have seen the book, have you, Creighton's *Harold Innis*? On return to me I passed on the correspondence to Queen's.

Did Innis have the Canadian intellect you most admired?
It is wrong to say intellect. I wasn't, shall I put it, bright enough to think in terms of an intellectual companionship any more than was the case with T.S. Eliot who became, at one time, a close friend. I didn't know anything about Eliot's poetry; I gave him low limericks and he liked them. Just a few months ago Lower said to me, "how the devil did you get on such close terms with Innis?" and I said it was a matter of chemistry. It is absurd to think that all academic associations are based on intellect. Creighton's relationship with Innis, I am sure, was chiefly intellectual. And they shared antipathies—always a great bond, because as soon as Innis realized that Creighton didn't like the u.s. or vice versa (afraid of its dominance), they became close friends. That was the beginning. There was no such relationship in my case with Innis. I thought in

some matters he was off course, particularly in his attitude towards the U.S. and in two or three other ways. In my obituary for the *Times*, I said there were certain issues in which it seemed to me he was dead wrong. The *Times* left out the word "dead," which I think was silly of them. It's a good English phrase: to be "dead wrong."

In regard to personal relationships it would be absurd to say that we ignored the "intellectual." He seemed to like what I wrote, and told me so, although I offered interpretations that he did not agree with. I am sure it was Innis who was the deciding force in getting me the Guggenheim Fellowship, despite his distrust of much of American practices. He had a basic suspicion of American policies. His was a sensitive nose that smelled corruption whether hidden in closet or council chamber. In *Sea Power and British North America 1783–1820* (published by Harvard shortly before the last war) I tried to say that certain policies were adopted by the state in pursuit of a national purpose, perhaps national security. Innis tended to see some corrupt merchant group pulling the strings behind the dark curtains. On that point, or points related to that problem, we often disagreed. But academic disagreements make no difference if you are bound close to a person. As the wise old lady who provided the money for the Parkin Scholarships said to me one time, one of the uses of a university education is that you learn to like people for what they are, not for what you want them to be. Not that I'd be so patronizing as to say I wanted Innis to be anything else but himself. Friendship is rarely based entirely on intellectual relationships.

It was obvious that you were quite close to him. I noticed the letters right up to the end.
Yes. His death was a frightful blow and it affects your life after-

wards. You think of what might have happened. The first thought, when W.L. Grant died: "who have I got to support me now?" In the long run, when you outgrow your callow youth, it is your turn to support somebody.

Did Innis ever come to your seminar?
I don't believe he ever did. I don't know why. A.L. Burt did, and even the mighty Tawney turned up once.[7]

I can understand that retirement did not drive you to the chimney-corner. You have spoken about a steady advance to "eastern approaches," and I notice that your last book was called *The China Station*, published in 1978. Was this the happy culmination of a plan that had gradually taken shape over the years? You may have been, as you once acknowledged, a European at heart, but the East seems to have drawn you like a magnet.
Yes. China had always fascinated me from childhood on. I had kept in touch with uncles and aunts who had been doctors, nurses, missionaries, and tea merchants in Canton, Fuchow, and Peking. I used to haunt the Chinese laundry in Markham, Ontario; its oriental curtains concealed, for me, mysteries as alluring as the odour of incense sticks. I was invited, as visiting professor, to the University of Hong Kong in 1966, and the bountiful Leverhulme Trust supported the venture, as did my ever-caring employers at King's. Under Leverhulme auspices, I returned to Hong Kong in 1973, once again to survey the Canton delta and neighbouring islands and put the last touches to my book. There was time to revisit Macao, explore the library, and afterwards to spend a week in Taiwan, where once again I lectured on the British Empire (of which I had witnessed the last stages), to the Academia Siniaca.

But *The China Station* was finished, and its publication marked my seventy-fifth birthday. Looking backward, it seemed to be the end of a very long trail, a trail followed by instinct rather than logical design, except in the latter stages. I had followed the Royal Navy from the North Atlantic to the Indian Ocean, and finally the China Sea. My travels had also encompassed the last days of the old British Empire.

The discussion then turned to Professor Graham's own views on the Empire.

As I said in the last part of the little book I referred to earlier, *Tides of Empire*, I think peoples who were part of the British empire and governed by the British benefited on the whole rather than lost. I use the phrase "I would hazard"; you will find that in the last lines of *Tides of Empire*. (That book has a bit about my boyhood, *Boys' Own Paper* stuff, with affectionate memories of the old British Empire.) But the word "Imperialist," as used today, suggests a longing to keep on expanding, if not conquering, which is, of course, nonsense. You can't change history, although you may try to distort it. There *was* an empire. How stupid it is to suggest that this was all wrong. The British Empire is as much of our past as, say, the Roman Empire, and that kind of rule was in those times accepted.

Incidentally, when I was at Harvard as a young instructor and tutor, I chose to teach Greek history, which was then very fashionable. In the thirties, democracy was all the rage in university circles, encouraged, no doubt, by the ominous rise of Nazism in Germany. The Greeks seemed to represent the finest model in democracy. I wish I had taken the second choice offered. The

Romans left marvelous monuments to their genius in almost all parts of the European and African world. Democracy has lost some of its splendour; it has been misused and misrepresented. In some places, especially in Africa, it is in tatters. At least the ruins of the Roman Empire are a testimony to beauty; they bear no marks of fraud or pretence.

Do you think as a Canadian occupying the Rhodes Chair that you perhaps had a greater attachment to the empire than an Englishman would have had at that stage?

Oh! It is impossible to say. Kenneth Dike, my first Nigerian PH.D. student, states in his introduction to my *Festschrift* that my predecessor, Vincent Harlow, had attachments to government and administration that may have affected his viewpoint. Such a bias, however unconscious, is possibly inevitable. I can only say that I was free of any political or governmental involvement of any sort; and I never wished to have any. But whatever the private associations, I hope one can always assume that the purveyor of imperial history is a professional, whether English, Australian, or Canadian. There *was* an empire, its role and fruits are still being assessed; and there is a lack of perspective in making moral judgments about the past in the light of the present. Indeed, judgments are occasionally reflected in attitudes towards the present. I am horrified at the comments and judgments of the Canadian press and members of the Canadian government on the South African problem, which cannot be simplified and certainly shouldn't be sentimentalized. Similarly I don't believe in being sentimentally critical about empire. Why should a present generation scorn two or three hundred years of history, when that was an accepted mode of national development? I think I have made clear to you that when I object to too much stress on regionalism in Canadian history (and I believe it has been overdone) I want to see the national element receive greater emphasis. But there is no reason why a proud nation should cut itself off from British history for patriotic reasons; history is history.

You wrote something in the *TLS* in the late sixties about the Canadian destiny, about the diminishing role of Canada and so forth. Do you think that part of the problem of Canada's diminishing role has to do with this nationalism and that we should think more in terms of being part of a larger unit?

I don't know about the word "diminishing" because as a colony Canada had no great role. You know they used to boast about Canada being the great interpreter between the u.s. and Britain. That was never true. That was just a bit of silly talk, but Canadians used to like to think that they were the interpreters and, as you know, they never really were. British ties with Washington were far closer than those between Ottawa and Washington. As for that "diminishing Canadian role," I never believed there was much to diminish. What bothers me is the effort made by Canadian politicians, in particular, to try and claim that they influence international policy without having the necessary national muscle. And I tried to outline that (if I may make a point of drawing it to your attention) in Mason Wade's book *Regionalism in Canada*. He was the editor. I wrote the last chapter, and in there I took a smack of L.B. Pearson's notion that without power you can be a moral influence in the world. This is just claptrap of the worst sort. And I have only recently noticed that a friend of mine, George Ignatieff, expressed what I regard as naïve views in pursuit of what he calls "peace-mongering." A laudable aim, no doubt, but again, the advocate seems to be trying to demonstrate that influence is possible without strength. And I understand they are sending a PEI man, former president of PEI University, to Europe, to advise various governments on how Canada can best be an influence for peace. You probably know more about this than I do.

To get back again to this business of striving for world influence on the part of Canada. She was for an interval a not inconsiderable influence immediately after the Second World War, when Canada emerged as the fourth industrial nation. Then for a moment there was power based on industry. But inevitably, when stability returned after the period of post-war reconstruction, when Japan started rebuilding and Germany starting rebuilding, that short-lived kind of eminence or prominence disappeared. The pretence of staying on top seemed to be chiefly on the part of the Liberals. Pearson was as much a muddler as Mackenzie Bowell in 1894. In regard to the article you speak about, on the front page of the *TLS*, I was attacked for linking Pearson with Diefenbaker as a political failure; both were failures as prime ministers. But to get back to the essence of my argument, it is the absurdity of trying to fortify Canadian nationalism by seeking world influence. Why bother? I suppose it is part of nationalism to seek global recognition but, unhappily, influence still depends on the possession of power. Red-blooded rhetoric may appear to lead Canada into the international limelight, but the high-toned moral aims tend to outpace Canada's strength.

I hope I can express myself more clearly, or intelligently, when I write. Certainly it is safer to write than to talk extemporaneously and be so recorded. Writing almost always involves rewriting, erasing, simplifying, changing things about. There is less room for exaggeration, and more chance of eliminating error.

Gerald Graham needs little editorial comment in concluding this chapter. His view of the empire, bound in with his teaching on the subject, is not that of an emotional commitment to a lost cause. Rather it is the view of a Canadian who felt comfortable within the framework of a larger world association of which Canada was a significant component. Graham's teaching, writing, and life experiences are an expression of the reality of what had been the British Empire/Commonwealth, but he was no less a Canadian for them. As the *Times* obituary put it, "to his British friends, he seemed an archetypal Canadian" (7 July 1988).

CHAPTER SEVEN

THE GENERATIONS SINCE 1945

The years immediately after the Second World War witnessed dramatic shifts in Canadian academic life. There was a huge influx of veterans into universities following demobilization. New professors had to be hired, at least temporarily, and the attitudes of faculty toward the subject-matter and teaching of history began to change. There was increasing interest in the more modern era, in Canadian as opposed to British and imperial history, and in social history instead of the constitutional and economic developments. Did such changes reflect the fall of the old imperial mentality or did they, in fact, through the generations of influential students who studied along the new lines, help to hasten it?

Certainly it can be argued that those who saw history, especially the Canadian variety, as the growth and progress of the constitution could not fail to appreciate Britain's relevance. Its constitutional developments were ours, its achievements were ours, its genius for governing was ours. The newer interests of the social historian, in the Canadian or British field, did not include exploration of such links. Indeed, in social history the peculiarities of locality have been a special feature. So too has the desire to move away from "élitist" concerns to the history of the "people."

Although Canadian history had been introduced as a regular subject in the days of George Wrong (who did not die until 1948), the complete separation of Canadian and British history had not taken place by 1945. Professors continued to teach both fields into the post-Second World War era and to relate the two. Gerald Graham perpetuated this tradition even up to 1970 while teaching at the University of London. By then, however, the divorce was complete almost everywhere in Canada.

The case of Maurice Careless is instructive in this regard. After taking undergraduate training at Toronto, where at one stage he was a member of the "young reactionaries" group in Frank Underhill's class, Careless went to Harvard to study under David Owen.[1] There his courses were mainly in British history, including instruction by Owen, Charles McIllwain, and Elliott Perkins as well as exposure to the broader cultural concepts of Crane Brinton and the "frontier thesis" ideas of the Americanist, Frederick Merk. Though his thesis was on George Brown and *The Globe*, it was conceived of as a study in mid-Victorian liberalism in a North American setting.[2] Later Careless drew upon his British and European knowledge, especially of the medieval period, in developing his famous metropolitan thesis in Canadian history. When he returned to Toronto in the late 1940s, he taught British history, phasing in his Canadian interests until in 1959 he finally gave up his course on eighteenth-century England.

One would expect that Canadians teaching Canadian history initiated the divorce proceedings, but this was not entirely so. Many

Canadian historians such as Donald Creighton and Charles Stacey emphasized, if not revered, the link. But the demands of the British field itself also forced many professors with twin interests to narrow their focus. In the post-Second World War period professors were also expected to be more serious about research in their primary field. Men of Frank Underhill's age were excused, for they had often done prodigious reading in the British field since their graduate years. Underhill kept remarkably detailed files on the latest articles and books in British history, even after retirement. Younger men, however, were expected to keep up with their counterparts at British (and American) universities who had begun to produce considerable numbers of books and articles by the 1950s. David Spring who, like Maurice Careless, had received his BA at Toronto and his PH.D. from Harvard, was one of the young lecturers toiling in the postwar University of Toronto history department. There he was confronted not only with hundreds of undergraduates in large pass courses, but also with the legacy of his own training at Toronto. As he stated in an interview:

> The two most influential men on me were Frank Underhill and Donald Creighton and in very different ways. Together they strengthened an ambivalence no doubt originally of my own making. . . . Underhill distinctly enhanced my feeling that history ought to be present minded and connected with teaching and citizenship. . . whereas Donald was fully immersed in research, so the research-scholar who was in me too was enhanced by him.[3]

About this time Spring became one of the first historians on either side of the Atlantic to examine the records of nineteenth-

century landed estate owners. His reputation as a scholar continuously grew thereafter. James Conacher, who started to teach in
the Tudor-Stuart area and then switched to Victorian English
politics, by the mid-fifties was writing to Underhill about his finds
in the mountain of Gladstone papers. At the other end of Canada,
however, John Norris at the University of British Columbia sub-
stantially began the trend toward publishing British history with
Lord Shelburne and Reform (1963). Norris religiously made his
way to England every May, after classes, to resume research.[4] His
regimen was soon followed by many other Canadian academics.

James Conacher recalled years earlier a query from Arthur
Lower about why Canadian professors did not publish in the British field despite the fact that so many taught it.[5] E.R. Adair made
more or less the same point for the entire non-Canadian area when
he wrote in 1943 "there has not been during the past fifty years, so
far as I know, one single work of real historical distinction produced by historians in Canada which does not deal with Canadian
history."[6] These queries had now been answered. For many historians, both British- and North American-trained, the English tradition of empirical research was to be satisfied directly—no longer
through the Canadian publishing route but through writing about
Britain itself. Research money and the greater ease of transatlantic
travel assisted these developments.

With the increasing dissolution of links between Canada and
Britain, the expansion of graduate studies in Canada necessitated
more research and publications. By the 1960s it had become more
difficult for professors at graduate seminars not to practise what
they preached. Canada was singularly blessed by a number of distinguished or soon-to-be distinguished scholars who would become
the leaders of research activity.

After 1945 Bertie Wilkinson became an outstanding authority on that older mainstay of history departments—English constitutional history. Despite admiring the achievements of English government in the High Middle Ages, Wilkinson in his many postwar volumes contributed sound analyses of the complexities of reconciling liberty and order. His seminar on the age of Wycliffe revealed the strong traditions of empiricism. Wilkinson was joined in his teaching by a younger Englishman, Michael Powicke. Powicke's mentor at Oxford had been his uncle, Sir Maurice Michael Powicke, who in turn had been one of Tout's pupils (Powicke was also born in Manchester). Powicke believes that Wilkinson's analysis of the role of monarchy, underestimated by many earlier liberal writers, was a great contribution to historiography. As a colleague he found Wilkinson to be both "friendly" and "critical" when the need arose.[7] Though secular-minded, Wilkinson also worked increasingly with colleagues at the Pontifical Institute at the University of Toronto. Like classics, medieval history found itself to be one of the earliest areas of sharply declining student interest by the 1960s. Given that many modern British historians treat history before Bosworth as a separate category, medievalists of all descriptions had many reasons to act in common. Wilkinson also assisted the work of the Ottawa-based private scholar, Margaret Labarge.

Wilkinson sometimes seemed too apologetic in his support of constitutional history, perhaps unyielding in the face of new approaches to history, which was understandable given the earlier emphasis placed on it by historians in Canada. Yet by the late 1960s he was accepting that one should understand the cultural origins of the British constitution. In this context Wilkinson, like other older historians, increasingly sympathized with the interdisciplinary work of the Pontifical Institute and helped to establish one of the jewels of the University of Toronto—the Centre for Medieval Studies.

Admittedly the Pontifical Institute was interested in medieval Europe as a whole, not simply Britain. However, many of the interests of faculty and the library resources focused attention on medieval England. The extensive microfilm copies of court rolls, account rolls, and other administrative documents, far more extensive than for any other country, made intensive primary research possible without one's having to leave Toronto. The records dictated some of the work of priest-scholars such as Michael Sheehan and Leonard Boyle (later the first North American to be appointed Vatican librarian). Ambrose Raftis made particularly important contributions to social and economic history in his publications about English villages in the late Middle Ages. Raftis, after obtaining his doctorate at Laval in the social sciences, had taken a second PH.D. under the direction of the eminent economic historian M.M. Postan, at Cambridge. This broad background allowed Raftis to employ skills from various fields in his careful analysis of English village life. Village reconstruction was then pursued fruitfully by others at the Pontifical Institute and the Centre for Medieval Studies, producing some of the distinct qualities of what one reviewer in *Past and Present* described as "the Toronto school."[8]

In the Tudor and Stuart period less impressive strides were made in the 1950s and early 1960s. This was partly because of individual circumstances and partly because there was no corresponding research centre to the Pontifical Institute. Donald McDougall at Toronto obviously found original research virtually impossible without the more modern portable tape-recording devices and special assistance now available to the handicapped. However, he continued to have his readers go through the latest books and articles in his field and so gave expert direction to honours and graduate seminar students.

In another discipline C.B. Macpherson of the University of Toronto political economy department began to instruct students at the graduate level in political theory in the 1950s. Many of the people analysed in his famous seminar on possessive individualism were taken from eighteenth- and nineteenth-century Britain. His book, *The Political Theory of Possessive Individualism*, made Macpherson a major authority on seventeenth-century English political developments and the origins of capitalist thought. Through his friendship with Christopher Hill and other Stuart specialists, as well as his own writings, he was seen in Great Britain primarily as a historian rather than as a political scientist, being made a fellow of the Royal Historical Society. Macpherson was unusual in this country in combining thorough historical studies with value judgments of institutions and concepts and suggested remedies for the future. One of his notable PH.D. students was Ed Broadbent, who produced a thesis on John Stuart Mill.

A.S.P. Woodhouse, another Toronto scholar outside the history department, also inspired historical research on seventeenth-century England by Canadians and others. His book *Puritanism and Liberty*, reprinted in 1950, established him as an authority on seventeenth-century England. As Hugh MacCallum, a current professor of English at the U of T, wrote about the book, "it remains an essential gateway to the modes of thought of the age."[9] Indeed, Woodhouse's thorough exploration of original texts in his seminars was good training ground for any historian and one PH.D. thesis in history was actually produced mainly under his direction

(it later became a book—John New, *Puritan and Anglican*). David
Spring as a student found Woodhouse far more an intellectual historian than a literary critic.[10]

Woodhouse's influence went far beyond the history students
who took courses from him. He also directly inspired the early
leaders of both the Mill and the Disraeli projects (described in the
next chapter). One of his major contributions was to bridge the gap
between English literature and history—once united but then separated by the establishment of history chairs. His devotion to the
ideals of the honours program are well remembered at University
College. He also made a lasting contribution to the Canadian academic community as a whole through the publication, with
Acadia's Watson Kirkconnell, of *The Humanities in Canada*
(1940). Not only did Woodhouse encourage more scholarship
(which, in his view, produced more *educated* men as well as
books), but recommended practical steps to reach that goal. In no
small measure his efforts resulted in the establishment of the Canada Council (ultimately the Social Science and Humanities Research Council of Canada) and its system of fellowships, research
grants, and publishers' subventions. One can now scarcely imagine life without these aids for academics in the humanities and social sciences in Canada.

Apart from John Norris at British Columbia, the eighteenth century was not thoroughly covered at most Canadian universities, being regarded, as John Beattie has put it, as a "luxury item."[11] Yet
the period was again surveyed in the writings and lectures of Vincent Wheeler Bladen, another member, like Macpherson, of the
Toronto Political Economy Department, though an economist.
Much of Bladen's teaching was in the grand tradition of economic
history that stretched back to Ashley. Eighteenth- and nineteenth-

century England was always important to him, as can be seen from his earliest books to *From Adam Smith to Maynard Keynes* (1974). The benefits of attending Bladen's classes were enormous. As C.B. Macpherson said, "the political theorist and professional historian are at a great advantage knowing economic history."[12]

Bladen embodied all the spheres of activity so admired by Wrong—he was a productive researcher, capable administrator, public servant, and good teacher. In the latter two areas there was exceptional achievement, as he was a prime supporter of the National Ballet School, serving on its board, and chairman (and sole member) of the Royal Commission on the Canadian Automotive Industry (1960–1) that provided the basis for the Auto Pact. He continued to teach as a special lecturer at Scarborough College long after he became an emeritus professor at the St. George campus of the University of Toronto. At seventy-three he insisted on teaching for free, for his Scarborough salary was, in his words, "ridiculously large" and there were "too many young men who can't get appointments."[13]

Another academic interested in the same period of history, who had a similar involvement in the arts and public service, was Hilda Neatby of the University of Saskatchewan. Neatby's association with Vincent Massey is a particularly good example of the historical profession in the service of the public interest. Born in England, Neatby as a girl moved to Saskatoon, where she earned her honours degree in history. She was deeply impressed there by the young Frank Underhill. Later she studied under another famous Canadian, A.L. Burt, at the University of Minnesota. Neatby wanted to teach British history because of the wider, interesting issues involved in the field. In scholarship, however, she did a great deal to promote the writing (and teaching) of Canadian history and

Canadian culture in general. She was highly influential when working on the Massey Commission (the Royal Commission on National Development in Arts, Letters and Sciences, 1949–51) and later was a personal adviser to Vincent Massey when he became the first Canadian-born governor-general.

Since his time at Toronto, Vincent Massey had maintained ties with the historical profession in Canada. As governor-general, however, his time for writing and reading was limited. Thus Neatby became both a confidante and a speechwriter. Recommending works by Creighton, Lower, and Brebner about Canada, she also advised Massey to read Larman Wymer's *Dr. Arnold of Rugby* and noted that *The Listener* was a "great source of inspiration."[14] Her own English background emerged on a number of occasions, including in one letter to Massey recounting an incident with a customs officer, who upon learning that she was born in England argued that she could not be a Canadian citizen.

But her point about English culture and the value of the Commonwealth was in part the result of her view of Canadian history and in part of her English background and experience teaching British history. In a memorandum on the "Anglo-Canadian Nexus" which accompanied a letter to Massey (22 December 1960), she reflected on the historic dialogue or "conversation" between the mother country and Canada in contrast to the American path to nationhood through revolution:

> The important thing is that this conversation went on, and went on in a totally different context from Anglo-American diplomatic dealings. It may be argued that Canada's development has been retarded by this association. That she has failed to see herself as a N. American Power. The answer

might be that even if this were so the delay is worth while. We have emerged with a modern constitution (compared with the rather archaic structure of the U.S.) and with the habit of natural association with countries in every part of the world—the only American (North or South) country to have acquired such a habit.

No one has commented (so far as I know) on Britain's remarkable feat of dissolving her Empire with an absolute minimum of disorder and bloodshed. Churchill refused to preside over a dissolution. Considering the record of France and Belgium, he might have been proud to do so. (p 2)

Once again the tradition of linking Britain to Canada through constitutional history can be seen. By then Neatby was already a celebrated figure in Canadian intellectual circles. *So Little for the Mind,* published in the early fifties, showed, in part, her disdain for American-style education and values associated with postwar prosperity. Like Massey, she preferred the orderly hierarchy of the older English-Canadian culture, which was patterned on the Old World, the latter being identified with *true* culture.[15] Back at Saskatchewan, Neatby was extremely influential in a department which produced two impressive historians of Britain—James McConica and Richard Rempel.

In the 1950s the University of Alberta also began to build a larger history department, including a strong contingent of British specialists. Lewis Gwynne Thomas was joined by W.J. Jones in the Tudor-Stuart field and Brian Heeney for the nineteenth century. As at Saskatchewan, such historians eventually could place their students in graduate studies in Britain and the United States

as readily as in central Canada. As the population and wealth of
the West advanced, the idea of indigenous graduate schools also
gained momentum. In the nineteenth-century field at Toronto, Underhill was succeeded briefly by Maurice Careless and then by
J.B. Conacher in the 1950s. Jim Conacher had taught British history at Toronto since 1946, but his early teaching experience had
been in the Tudor area, while he edited works of Canadian history.
By the late 1950s he had made the transition to Victorian England
and through graduate teaching and research, in Maurice Careless's
words, "powerfully forwarded the redevelopment of British Studies
in Canada."[16] Conacher's eventual volumes on mid-Victorian
politics had earned him an international reputation by the 1970s.
Long before that, Conacher students such as Peter Marsh,
Christopher Kent, Robert Stewart, and others had been inspired to
build careers in the same field.

The study of the nineteenth century at Toronto also profited by
the arrival of A.P. Thornton in 1959. A Scotsman educated at Oxford, Thornton had been head of the history department at the University of the West Indies. This interest and practical experience
in living in what was left of the Empire was confirmed in his important work, *The Imperial Idea and Its Enemies*. Describing himself
as more of an "ideas man than an archives man," Thornton advo-
cated careful examination of the "mentalité" of British imperialism
(without the full implications of the Annales school terminology).[17]
His subsequent publications as well as his stimulating method of
conducting seminars put Toronto on the map as a centre for the
study of British imperialism. Thornton's books also represented an
important milestone in the development of modern intellectual and
cultural history in Canada.

Canadians also continued to be important professors of imperial history abroad during this period. Their number included Gerald Graham at London and Richard Preston at Duke, who taught Canadian history as part of imperial history. Another Canadian, C.M. MacInnes, was professor of imperial history at Bristol until 1957. Born in Calgary and educated at Dalhousie and Balliol, Oxford, MacInnes joined the Bristol history department in 1919. "Mac," as he was called, had been blind since early childhood. Despite this handicap, he produced four historical books about the empire, another on Bristol, one on the Canadian cattle country (*In the Shadow of the Rockies*, 1930). He also edited a number of historical collections. Mac even wrote adventure stories for young people and some verse translations from French, Dutch, and German for the BBC. As an academic, he was not only a concerned teacher but also dean of arts, editor of the journal of the Association of University Teachers, and founder in 1936 of a university discussion club that still exists. It is not surprising that Bristol commissioned a bronze head of Mac from Epstein. Decorated by The Netherlands government for war work, he also received honorary degrees from Dalhousie and Alberta.[18] Charles MacInnes was truly a remarkable man.

At McGill there was also much activity in the nineteenth-century field. Stanford Reid returned to the pulpit of Fairmount Taylor Presbyterian Church in 1941 fresh with a PH.D. from the University of Pennsylvania. Invited to do some teaching by principal Cyril James, Reid replaced Fryer in teaching modern British and modern European history. Though his original field was the Reformation, Reid subsequently supervised work running into the nineteenth century, including Hereward Senior's well-known thesis and book on Orangeism in the British Isles. Though they were not all in British history, Reid remembers supervising eigh-

teen MA and PH.D. students at the same time: "When I was running the residences I used to have Thursday afternoon as my afternoon for Graduate Students. At 2 o'clock the MA and PH.D. students would meet, that is the ones in certain fields would meet,
and then at 3:30 we would have refreshments and then another
group would come in and then I would go on with them until 5
o'clock."[19] Reid subsequently introduced Celtic history to the curriculum, which formed the basis of a Scottish studies program he
later founded at Guelph.

The head of the McGill department after the war, Noel Fieldhouse, also taught some British history but confined it largely to
European diplomatic history. Fieldhouse was also increasingly involved with public affairs, as he had been at Manitoba, being a frequent platform speaker. A staunch conservative, he had some interesting public debates with Frank Scott and has become somewhat of a cult figure in recent years for many on the political Right.
Subsequently, as dean of arts, he had an important impact on attitudes toward history as a discipline at McGill and elsewhere. His
views on the nature of history were clear and to the point, as
revealed in this internal university memorandum:

> It is not the purpose of history to serve as the factual mate-
> rial for a generalising social science. It aims, rather, to
> provide man with a knowledge of himself. It shows man
> what he is by showing him what he has done. The critical
> re-experiencing of the thought involved in *res gestae* en-
> larges and enlightens the mind bringing before it the vari-
> ety of human nature. History in this respect is akin to liter-
> ature, and belongs properly with the humanities.[20]

Although Fieldhouse expressed many sound views on the nature of history, pressure mounted in the next decades to include it within social science. Though many historians probably would have been reluctant to join the positivists, distrusting the claim that history was a science, granting agencies tended to move the practitioner into that camp. As in the United States and Britain, topic introversion and "tunnel history" were the natural products of the graduate seminar in the 1960s and 1970s. However, the breakdown of British history into highly specialized courses related to professors' research interests could not be accomplished in most Canadian schools to the degree seen in Britain during the same period.

Before the complete establishment of graduate programs at many major schools in Canada by 1970, there continued to be the possibility of study abroad. Although study in Britain became less fashionable, there was always the American graduate route. Here Canadians also made significant contributions. Among the leading United States supervisors of undergraduate and graduate research in British history, Canadian expatriates took an inordinate share of the honours. They included not only J.B. Brebner at Columbia but also David Spring at Johns Hopkins, A.L. Burt at Minnesota, and Goldwin Smith at Wayne State.

Though his publications were almost all in the Canadian field, A.L. Burt for many years had been known as the British historian at Minnesota and was ensconced there. Both Preston and Spring ended up in the United States by personal choice in the late 1940s.

At Wayne State a group of Canadians also interested in British history, like the earlier clustering of Brebner, Shotwell, and Peardon at Columbia, had appeared. They included Frederick Coyne

Hamil (1903–68), who taught both Canadian and British constitutional history at the Detroit school, and the better-known Goldwin Smith. Born in Siloam, Ontario, and a graduate of both Western and Toronto, Smith completed his PH.D. where the other Goldwin Smith had once taught—Cornell. His name caused more than one problem in cashing cheques in Ithaca because of the famous Goldwin Smith Hall.[21] After stints at Missouri and Iowa, Smith joined the Wayne State faculty in 1947. His subsequent publications in general British history, as well as in constitutional history and Tudor political and social history, were significant. Smith also wrote extensively about educational questions and continued to exhibit interest in Canadian history through articles and reviews. He did much to build up the Conference on British Studies, which later was led by one of his former students, Martin Havran, a distinguished Canadian professor of early modern British history at Virginia.

In teaching British history, as other areas of history, Canadian schools moved more toward the American model than to the British at the graduate level. With the possible exception of McGill, most universities opted for increased course and field exams and foreign-language requirements prior to students' embarking on the PH.D. thesis. Toronto in the mid- and late 1960s seemed to be a hybrid of the British and American models, with course and examination hurdles similar to those in American graduate schools, but with a lengthy, original thesis taking some years to complete. By that time most PH.D. theses required work in British archives. As Wilfrid Cude in *The Ph.D. Trap* (1987) has suggested, the rites of passage to the PH.D. can become extremely lengthy.

At the undergraduate level, much of the élitism of the old days began to collapse. Maurice Careless could still remember the lessons in social etiquette Ralph Flenley gave into the 1950s to honours students at his home on the behaviour of "British gentlemen."[22] Elliot Rose thought that Toronto was more like the Britain of twenty years earlier when he arrived in the early 1950s from Cambridge.[23] "Afternoon tea" was still taken by the Toronto history department for a few years after the move to new quarters in 1961, though the custom did not last long after that.

More substantial than all this change was the dismantling of the honours program at Toronto as a result of C.B. Macpherson's report at the end of the 1960s. The system, so admired by Wrong and others, was to be no more. But earlier developments had shown that the tide was changing. When Donald Creighton was chairman in the 1950s, newer national areas of history were added that made the specific area and period requirements of the old system less feasible. Tutorials were also given to general students by the late 1950s, thus blurring the rigid distinctions between general and honours students that had been true previously. Other universities, however, even some close by such as McMaster, did not always follow in Toronto's footsteps and did not abolish the honours system.

Canadian history was also increasingly detached from remaining links with British history. Teachers such as Kenneth McNaught began to think that a continental perspective was the best way to place Canadian history in a wider context. Given these various changes, British history often, unfairly, was regarded with hostility by advocates of change. Guilt by association was the major "sin" of British history in the early 1970s. However, unlike in Britain itself, the field at least did not *suffer* from the mercurial interest of those who moved toward what was trendy or politically relevant. After the de-emphasis on constitutional history, it became obvious that British history was losing ground as an important field, let alone as a centrepiece of historical studies in Canada. Withering Commonwealth relationships also indicated for some its political irrelevance, and the influx of non Canadian professors brought a certain detachment to teaching of the subject. One suspects that it now began to be taught in Canadian universities in a way that would not be so different from that in Maine or Arizona.

CHAPTER EIGHT

CONTEMPORARY TEACHING AND RESEARCH

Despite its generally altered status since the Second World War and declining enrolment in it in the early 1970s, British history has remained a popular subject in Canadian higher education. As J.B. Conacher noted in his 1975 presidential address to the Canadian Historical Association, there was a marked increase in graduate studies in non-Canadian fields, British history having by far the largest number of theses produced.[1] At the undergraduate level, survey and specialist courses attract sufficient numbers to ensure their continued existence and recently have received more takers than in the last decade or so.

Such a situation begs explanation. First, as Albert Tucker of York University has indicated, there is intrinsic interest in the subject-matter itself.[2] Some professors have noted that students have more diverse ethnic backgrounds, particularly in large urban centres, compared to the small, predominantly Anglo-Saxon variety of twenty-five years ago. For these students a certain objectivity may have increased their appetite for the subject. Anglo-Saxon students may have found the overly familiar theme of the British heritage wearing a bit thin by the late 1960s. Both students and professors of Canadian history recently have had renewed reason to delve into the history of Britain as the cradle of so many economic, cultural, and intellectual trends, quite apart from politics, which are important to this country. With some ebbing in the force of Canadian nationalism since the 1960s reappraisal of the importance of British history may have helped to increase enrolment figures in some universities. The continental approach to Canadian history also has had drawbacks. In limiting the scope of American influence on our history we may invite a re-emphasis on British traditions which had become unfashionable.

There are also more negative factors at work. With the decline of foreign-language requirements and skills at the college level, those not interested in North America and wishing to pursue graduate studies naturally gravitate toward British history. Teaching opportunities at the college level are better, when one considers the number of professors of British history outside Canada compared, for example, with those in the Canadian studies. Some increasing interest in "theme" fields and courses crossing national fields, such as "urbanization," at the graduate level also have tended to embrace more British history, though not formally by that name.

In Quebec universities, interest in British history has increased, possibly because of its less sensitive nature, being no longer identified with Anglo ascendancy in Canada. Even more than this, the availability of texts and specialized monographs in French has been greatly increased. It has always been obvious to those whose native tongue is not English that the study of British history is useful, if only in explaining how the English language developed. The student and teacher of English literature should be that much more convinced of its worth. The language itself, one suspects, will always sustain a reasonable level of interest in British history.

Recently, Cambridge historian David Cannadine wrote about the decline in teaching of British history in British universities.[3] In recounting this tale of woe, Cannadine speaks of a Golden Age of professional excitement in the fifties and sixties when the themes of revolutionary change throughout Britain's history, as revealed in writing and teaching, seemed to make Britain the pace-setter for all modern trends in the eyes of students, a view which Cannadine feels was "Whiggish" and too "present-minded."[4] While some of these notions might have appealed to Canadians, their background was hardly that of "the new comprehensives and campuses of the welfare state," nor did they crowd into British history courses in the sixties.[5] The older emphasis on constitutional history may have made many young Canadians feel that British history was old-fashioned. In the rebellious campus days of the late 1960s and early 1970s, as Harry Granter of Dalhousie suggests, the British story of the growth of political stability even deterred those interested primarily in current events from enrolling.[6] By the 1970s, social history and the history of disadvantaged groups created interest in new fields among those taking British history courses.

At this point, perhaps the greatest danger of fragmenting the field occurred in North America, not only in British history, but in all fields. The noted British historian at the City University of New York, Gertrude Himmelfarb, wrote recently about the dangers of these approaches in *The New History and the Old* (1987). There was no comparable bust in the market in British history by the late 1970s as there had never been a boom. Of necessity, studies of narrow areas of British history for the most part had not occurred in Canada. At most universities the lecture method continued to be used because a complete seminar or tutorial system, in the English sense, seemed impractical and too expensive. Wide survey courses, largely within a political framework, persisted. The fragmentation of general, national themes in teaching the subject, as Cannadine suggests for Britain, never took place to any great extent in Canada at the undergraduate level. As noted in Chapter 1, Canadians have been conspicuous for the production of textbooks as well as broad works of synthesis such as *The Great Arch* (1985) by sociologists Philip Corrigan of the Ontario Institute for Studies in Education and Derek Sayer of the University of Alberta.

Research, of course, has been important. In the medieval area the Toronto Centre for Medieval Studies has produced a number of PH.D's, many employing techniques derived from other disciplines, in detailed examinations of social and cultural life. At the Pontifical Institute the art of village society reconstitution, inspired by Ambrose Raftis, has attracted international attention. More traditional forms of research, perhaps less detailed, on the Middle Ages have been continued, including those in the Bertie Wilkinson tradition. A particular strength of the Toronto centre has been its ability to draw upon different disciplines, not simply for research techniques, but also for teaching. The interdisciplinary approach in general has helped to stimulate interest in other areas of British history at Canadian universities.

Almost at the other end of the time-frame, the nineteenth century has benefited particularly from the interdisciplinary approach. In the mid-1960s interest in social and intellectual history began to mount, assisted by the appearance of a new generation of professors. The Victorian Studies Association of Ontario was founded, and was followed shortly after, by the interdisciplinary English and history MA program in Victorian studies, established jointly by Toronto and York universities. In both cases British historians benefited greatly from affiliation with the much larger number of English literature specialists working in the field. Historians such as R.J. Helmstadter also contributed their considerable knowledge of a wide range of social, intellectual, and political topics to training literature students. Such cross-fertilization, in terms of organizations, has seldom resulted in such successes in the United States or the United Kingdom. One factor for success in this case was the greater likelihood that the historian would have some training in literature because of the longer time spent on undergraduate and graduate education in Canada compared, for example, with Britain.

In western Canada a similar organization to the VSAO was formed in the 1970s with an even more ambitious annual program of papers and publications. Historians might well have believed that the stretching necessary to make such joint enterprises work was due mainly to their efforts, but doubtless someone in English literature would see it differently. Somewhat distinct from the activities of the graduate programs and associations has been the institution of interdisciplinary "megaprojects" focused on modern England, the foremost being the Mill project.

The idea of an up-to-date collection of the writings of John Stuart Mill originated in the 1950s with John Robson, then completing his PH.D. thesis in English at Toronto. As an undergraduate, Robson was enrolled in the engineering and physics program, then became an honours psychology student, and completed the general honours program in his last two years. Before proceeding to his MA and PH.D., therefore, he did a "make-up"

year in English and was exposed to the influence of A.S.P. Woodhouse. Eventually working in areas that could be classified as intellectual history, Robson concluded that Mill deserved a series of
edited volumes. Woodhouse supported the idea and helped to persuade the University of Toronto Press to publish the resulting
volumes. The project began in 1959 with F.E.L. Priestley as general editor, Robson succeeding to the position thirteen years later.
Throughout the years, however, Robson was the textual editor,
which provided continuity in the everyday aspects of the work.
Needless to say, the project has taken longer than anticipated,
there being twenty-six years of editorial work and twenty volumes
thus far. Even such straightforward items as reproducing a speech
given in the House of Commons could reveal the inadequacy of
such revered sources as *Hansard*.[7] New types of footnotes, such as
those for newspapers, had to be devised. Along the way a small
cottage industry surrounding Mill appeared. The *Mill Newsletter*
has been a central source for the dissemination of knowledge about
current research on the English intellectual. Jack Robson has become perhaps the world's foremost authority on his life-long subject.

The success of the Mill project has inspired similar ventures.
Like the Mill project, the Disraeli project had humble beginnings
and ambitions at Queen's University in 1972. The founders of the
project were J.P. Matthews of the English department and historian Donald Schurman. Schurman had become interested in Disraeli both as a result of his teaching in the imperial field and his
personal experience of having stayed once in Disraeli's house at
Hughenden. Matthews was also interested in Disraeli from the
Commonwealth perspective, having been born in Australia and
educated there and at the University of Toronto. Here, as in the

Mill project, the influence of Woodhouse could be seen, for Matthews had been one of his students.

As Matthews and Schurman both had sabbatical leaves in 1972–3, they united in a modest project to produce a selected edition of Disraeli's speeches and letters. It was believed at the time that only 2,500 letters had survived into the late twentieth century. Matthews, who was in charge of collecting letters, spent his leave at Oriel College, Oxford. There, after conversations with Lord Blake, Disraeli's current biographer, he learned that recent books had relied on the same letters originally used by Buckle in the first biography. Upon visiting Lord Bradford in Shropshire, however, he discovered that only a small portion of the Bradford letters had been released by his grandfather at the end of the First World War. As all of those mentioned directly or indirectly in the withheld letters were now dead, Matthews was given access to more than 1,500 pieces of correspondence not seen by historians. This led him to believe that there were many more letters to be found in a large number of collections. This hunch proved to be correct.

In many cases Matthews discovered that tales of destruction by drunken butlers, careless maids, or disastrous fires were often fictions undoubtedly designed to put off overzealous American researchers. Dizzy's success with ladies probably on occasion led to the destruction of correspondence. Nevertheless, a vast collection was unearthed.

One of the most interesting finds was at Windsor Castle. In the last century there had been rumours of an affair between Disraeli and the widowed Queen Victoria, as well as a story that the correspondence had been destroyed by Edward VII. Upon contacting the royal archivist at Windsor, Matthews was permitted to examine

BRITAIN'S PAST IN CANADA

a great deal of hitherto unpublished Disraeli material in the sovereign's personal archives. Permission to have these microfilmed was granted by the Queen.[8]

Detective work was extremely important. Uncatalogued private deposit collections (for which there was sometimes uncertainty about who held the rights to letters) were hard to discover at major repositories. Even bizarre locations could not be overlooked, such as Disraeli's coal bin at Hughenden, which yielded a canvas bag filled with his awards and other memorabilia! By the time editing had begun it was clear that the project was much larger than had been anticipated. Matthews and Schurman were joined by two more Queen's faculty — J.A.W. "Jock" Gunn of the political science department and Melvin Wiebe from English. Canada Council assistance allowed the project to have an appropriate staff size. The University of Toronto Press began to publish volumes in 1982, by which time a Disraeli newsletter and an international symposium had been produced at Queen's. Reviews of the early volumes were very favourable on both sides of the Atlantic. Only the *Montreal Gazette* (4 December 1982) writer seemed to think Kingston, Ontario, an unlikely centre for Disraeli scholarship!

There is some irony in this latter view, for Disraeli had a number of Canadian connections, including being an adviser on Conservative policy to then Prime Minister Sir John A. Macdonald (and earlier at the time of the Durham Report). Matthews also recounts a number of instances where useful material was collected in Canada. On one occasion in early 1974, after reading an article in the *Whig Standard*, a worker at Alcan in Kingston approached the editors. A fellow steel worker in Hamilton claimed to have Disraeli letters. Later it was learned that the person in Hamilton was Sir Derek Hart Dyke, who did indeed have Disraeli correspondence. In nearby Port Hope, the headmaster of Trinity College School helped secure the correspondence of Lady Ely, often an emissary between Queen Victoria and Disraeli. The headmaster was the current Marquis of Ely. The Nova Scotia Archives yielded three letters and more may be found, though cross-referencing of Canadian archives collections would be helpful.

The editors have taken care not to be restrictive. Despite an inhibiting total of 17,000 letters uncovered to date, many are potentially of considerable significance and have been included for publication (though not those dictated). In this respect Jock Gunn has been most diligent. Students have also benefited from the microfilmed and original materials, three completed PH.D. theses having utilized them so far.

For Canada, Disraeli has remained a source of special interest both for the Empire/Commonwealth ideal and conservatism. People such as John Diefenbaker have been very supportive of the project for such reasons.

The Russell project at McMaster began with an initially grander scheme, with the purchase of the Bertrand Russell Papers at auction in England in the late 1970s. Russell was a major twentieth-century figure who had an enormous impact upon philosophy, science, and political thought. The acquisition of his papers made McMaster a unique centre for research, generating a newsletter, PH.D. theses, and the like. Negotiations and funding for the papers came from a variety of sources, including Cyrus Eaton, a McMaster graduate, Cleveland industrialist, and advocate of world peace. Opposition to the loss of a "national treasure" was considerable within Britain.[9] Alwyn Berland, then dean of humanities at McMaster, launched the editorial project after acquisition of the papers and since 1980, with Social Science and Humanities Research Council of Canada support, a number of volumes have been published by Allen and Unwin in Britain. Unlike the Mill project, different experts have appeared on the scene from time to time to give editorial advice, including John Passmore, the Australian philosopher, and the McMaster archivist Kenneth Blackwell, who knew Russell personally. Because Russell had such a complex mind, there have been special demands for unique editorial skills such as knowledge of analytical philosophy and mathematical theory. There have also been restrictions on the use of some letters until the death of Russell's own children. At McMaster, Richard Rempel of the history department and Andrew Brink of English and Nicholas Griffin of philosophy have provided continuity on the editorial team.

Rempel returned to Canada in 1975 and was part of the original faculty group linked to the project. Strongly influenced by Hilda Neatby, his English history professor at Saskatchewan, Rempel went on to do a D.Phil. at Oxford, focusing on divisions within the Unionist party over tariff reforms, which later was published. In 1964 he began his teaching career at the University of South Carolina, supervising some ten PH.D. theses in his years there. Rempel had been interested in Russell, perhaps stimulated in part by the existence of some papers of another British pacifist housed at South Carolina—Clifford Allen. In any case, Rempel had retained his Canadian citizenship and succeeded Bert McCready as the modern British specialist at McMaster in 1975. The project goes on.

It is impossible to explain why Canada has been the home of three such distinguished projects. Apart from good luck and the special initiative of individuals, these projects in part represent the rebuilding of bridges between disciplines rent apart by the

early establishment of specific chairs of English, history, and political science. Government funding provided through the Social
Science and Humanities Research Council of Canada and Canada
Council grants also sees the fulfilment of the earlier dream of
Brebner, Woodhouse, and others that the state would foster the
growth of enterprises that would place Canada in the forefront of
scholarly activity.

Of course, much of the research activity and scholarly publications in Canada has *not* been the result of team efforts or interdisciplinary activity. The early modern period was blessed by an
assortment of very talented historians from coast to coast. In the
Tudor-Stuart field, J.S. Jones, J.R. Lander (late medieval, early
Tudor), Elliot Rose, the late James Daly, Michael Maxwell, Paul
Christianson, and Michael Finlayson have been joined by younger
historians such as David Levine, all of whom have produced an
impressive array of important monographs. Those outside history
departments also continue to make contributions, such as the respected political theorist J.A.W. Gunn.

One must cite in this field the contributions of Father James
McConica. Like Rempel, he was a product of Saskatchewan, being
influenced in particular by Hilda Neatby and Charles Lightbody.
After having a Rhodes scholarship at Oxford and doing some study
in both the United States and Canada (including publication of an
article in Canadian history), McConica returned to Oxford in 1963
to complete his D.Phil. thesis under the supervision of Hugh
Trevor-Roper. His thesis on "The Continuity of Humanist Ideas
during the English Reformation" became the basis for further work
in the Renaissance-Reformation period. McConica's principal interest has been the interaction between social change and intellectual culture, especially how people perceive and explain

change. Though a convert to Roman Catholicism and a Basilian priest, he sees himself as an intellectual, cultural historian approaching religious topics rather than an historian of Catholic culture.[10] His books, articles, and work as an editor of both the Erasmus project and the official history of Oxford University and as a founder of the journal *Renaissance and Reformation* have earned McConica awards and honours inside and outside Canada. Currently president of St. Michael's College in Toronto, he has had the distinction of being elected a Fellow of All Souls, Oxford, as well as of the Royal Society of Canada.

For the eighteenth century, Canada has been well served since the pioneering publications of John Norris. John Money, Sydney Jackman, Donald Ginter, Karl Schweizer, J.B. Owen, Paul Fritz, George Rudé (in his Concordia period), Robert Malcolmson, Nicholas Rogers, and the political scientist J.B. Stewart have published important works and also inspired student interest in a field often uncomfortably wedged between the ever-expanding literature on the Stuart and Victorian periods. Many valuable exchanges have also come from the Early Modern English Group, who have been meeting regularly in southern Ontario since 1981.

One person who has had a remarkable impact on eighteenth-century studies is John Beattie of Toronto. Born in a coalmining area near Newcastle, England, Beattie moved with his parents to California when he was seventeen. There he attended the University of San Francisco on a soccer scholarship, pursuing studies in chemistry for two years and enjoying the company of a number of famous basketball and football stars. In his last two years at the Jesuit school, Beattie squeezed in a sufficient number of history courses to graduate with a major in his new-found interest. Here the inspiration of teachers such as Donald Campbell was very important.

An even greater influence on the young Beattie was George Guttridge, his mentor at Berkeley. Guttridge, an old Yorkshireman, inspired his students in every way with his gentlemanly humanity. As Beattie recalls, virtually all his students respectfully referred to him as "Mr. Guttridge."[11] He not only sparked Beattie's interest in the eighteenth century (he was a Burke scholar), but also to some degree aided Beattie's quest for personal identity being, like his mentor, neither quite a Californian nor an Englishman. It was perhaps inevitable that Beattie would move on to Guttridge's own school, Cambridge, though he had started PH.D. work at Berkeley.

Unlike many North Americans (with notable exceptions such as Gerald Graham), Beattie did well in the unstructured program for the PH.D. His supervisor was the well-known eighteenth-century historian J.H. Plumb, who strongly encouraged research, though not through frequent meetings or close personal contact with his graduate student. In developing his interest in the court system and its role in politics under George I, Beattie also encountered L.B. Namier who, of course, was anxious to support the "prosopographic" approach (though Namier may never have used the term himself). Romney Sedgwick and John Brooke also expressed interest, but in the latter's case the involvement with the history of Parliament project placed him in the Namier camp. Plumb, on the other hand, was resistant to Namier's approach and so the young PH.D. student's path was not altogether easy. Despite some nervousness about the high rate of non-completion among Cambridge PH.D.'s, Beattie did graduate, defending his thesis be-

fore a three-member board which included a future professor of
history and dean of arts at St. Mary's University in Nova Scotia—
the late J.B. Owen.

Through his thesis work and *The English Court in the Reign of
George I*, Beattie was concerned mainly with teaching political and
administrative history at Toronto (he arrived in 1961) in the older
tradition. By 1967, however, he had begun to move toward social
history. His approach initially was restrained, as he wished to
write about the attitudes of the gentry who controlled local
government—basically an institutional history set more in the
wider society. However, the recent work of seventeenth-century
historians in broadening the scope of political and administrative
studies had impressed him. Plunging into the particularly good
county records of Surrey, Sussex, and Wiltshire, Beattie found a
wide range of material in Quarter Sessions. He had decided to
focus on crime before such an interest became fashionable among
historians. This led to the application of ideas from sociology and
in time one of the earliest Canada Council-supported computer
projects. In order to study property crime and violence, Beattie became interested in "how things work" in the courts, that is, basically how jurors and judges responded to crime. In time, Beattie
was invited by the Centre for Criminology at the University of
Toronto to teach a course on crime from the historical perspective,
which was also open to law students. The result was a number of
papers on eighteenth-century English crime and one short book on
crime and punishment in Canadian history. The final product of
twenty years' labour has been the transatlantic publication of the
magisterial *Crime and the Courts* (1986) which has earned the Ger-
shoy Prize of the American Historical Association and the Wallace
K. Ferguson Prize from the Canadian Historical Association.

In talking with John Beattie one is always struck by his concern for the student. An outstanding graduate supervisor, he has taught a host of important scholars such as Robert Malcolmson, Nicholas Rogers, Peter Munche, Donna Andrew, and others. Yet he has always been concerned with the "jelly-like" quality of eighteenth-century studies, which might encourage administrators to see it as a "luxury" field in times of financial constraint—hence Beattie's worry about PH.D.s not getting appointments after graduation. No man has done more to make eighteenth-century British history an established field in this country.

As mentioned earlier, much in the way of association and project activity has characterized the Victorian field in Canada. However, there is such a large contingent of researchers in this area that individual enterprise has gone in all sorts of directions. Political history has been well served by J.B. Conacher at Toronto and James Winter at the University of British Columbia, both launching graduate students on promising careers. R.J. Helmstadter of Toronto has supervised a large number of PH.D. theses in social and religious history. Hereward Senior at McGill likewise has done admirable graduate thesis supervision in English and Irish history. Saskatchewan's Christopher Kent continues to make important contributions to Victorian intellectual history as well as being a founding member of the Victorian Studies Association of Western Canada. At Manitoba, social history, especially popular recreations, has received attention from Peter Bailey and Keith Sandiford, the latter having written a book on politics and diplomacy in an earlier stage of his career. James Lorimer at Wilfrid Laurier (like Bailey, a British Columbia PH.D.), has written an important book on Victorian racism. Angus McLaren at Victoria has made important contributions in the field of Victorian birth

control and sexuality. Interests in imperial matters have been well
served by J.K. Chapman and Murray Young (both former Graham
students) at New Brunswick, Trevor Lloyd at Toronto, Alan Adamson
son at Concordia, Arthur Keppel-Jones at Queen's, Michael
Craton at Waterloo, and John Flint (also trained by Graham) and
his associates at Dalhousie. Other specialties include the study of
newspapers by J.O. Stubbs, formerly of Waterloo (now president of
Trent), economic history by David Moss at Alberta, and parliamentary
politics by R.H. Cameron at St. Mary's and F.A. Dreyer
at Western. The history of science has benefited from the work of
M.P. Winsor and Trevor Levere at Toronto. Military history has
been covered by York's Albert Tucker and Trent's Patricia
Morton. Ann Robson of Toronto has made important contributions
on factory legislation, John Stuart Mill, and women's studies. The
latter field is also particularly well served by Carleton's Deborah
Gorham, Patricia Malcolmson of Kingston, Kathleen McCrone at
Windsor, and, on the religious side, by the late Brian Heeney at
Trent.

One interesting note on research is the apparent willingness of
an inordinately large number of historians to delve into the workings
of religion. In his 1987 Canadian Historical Association
keynote address, Canadian-born world historian W.H. McNeill
urged historians to give due weight to the role of religion as a significant
force in modern history. Many scholars publishing in British
studies in Canada seem to have chosen this path some time
ago. For the more recent past this includes R.J. Helmstadter, P.T.
Marsh, M. Johnson, Jacob Ellens, Paul Phillips, Peter Allen,
Roger Hutchison, Ian Newbould, Richard Schiefen, John P.B.
Kenyon, Thomas McIntrye, Bernard Lightman, Merrill Distad,
Sydney Eisen, Frederick Dreyer, Desmond Bowen, N. Cooper,

D.R. Pugh, Eugene Fairweather, W.S.F. Pickering (while in Canada), as well as Stanford Reid, M.P. Maxwell, and Donald Akenson for the "Celtic Fringe." John W. Grant also made an early contribution to the field (*Free Churchmanship in England, 1870-1940*) before turning his research energies to the Canadian scene. One might also note that James McConica, Ian Gentles, Michael Finlayson, Elliot Rose, P.K. Christianson, and John Morgan have produced significant writings on religion for the early modern period. Why there has been a particularly strong tradition of interest in religion and its social role among scholars in Canada is not easily explained but it is most welcome.

The twentieth century has received good coverage despite the reluctance of some scholars to consider anything after the First World War as history. Authorities in the field include Toronto's Trevor Lloyd and Sydney Aster, Western's Neville Thompson, McGill's Martin Petter, Montreal's Trevor Burridge, PEI's Donald Cregier, the late Peter Fraser of Dalhousie, and two political scientists—Michael Kinnear of Manitoba and the late R.T. Mackenzie of the London School of Economics. Most have made their reputations by analysing political developments.

Lastly, complaints made that British history is too English in its orientation have received a positive response by the Scottish studies program initiated by Stanford Reid at Guelph and carried on by E.J. Cowan, R.M. Sunter, and W.W. Straka, as well as the work done by Irish scholars at various universities, the most notable being the prolific writer, Donald Akenson, of Queen's.

Lest the reader see the contemporary scene as dominated by the researcher, it is important to point out that the older desire of the historian to influence the public mind and engage in issues of the day lives on. Whether in public lectures as invited speakers, letters to the editor, or as guests on television programs (Elliot Rose remembers being asked to be an annual Hallowe'en guest on the "Pierre Berton Show" following publication of *Razor for a Goat*), historians have accepted invitations to address the public. [12] As one experienced academic once said to me, "the historian must not refuse an audience." At times this has been an opportunity to contribute the special perspective of the historian, such as John Beattie's in a televised panel discussing criminology issues several years ago. On other occasions it has had more to do with the sense of commitment to particular causes. Trevor Lloyd, for example, has shared his perspective on social democracy in both Britain and Canada. Stanford Reid has preached from the pulpit on Sundays. At the lectern Reid did not disguise his own view of religious developments in certain areas of modern history, but rather saw the study of religion as a stimulus to further discussion inside and outside the classroom. Manitoba's Keith Sandiford has contributed to Black studies, being possibly the first Black to receive a PH.D. in history in this country. The late James Daly of McMaster dealt with broad educational questions, as in his critical study of the Hall-Dennis Report, *Education or Molasses?* (1969).

Occasionally it has been impossible to be both a pure historical scholar and a commentator on public issues—the "schizoid" condition described by David Spring. About the time he produced his book *Nuclear Disparities*, for example, Robert Malcolmson found it better to move into a new interdisciplinary field at Queen's while furthering his anti-nuclear war activism. [13] In this move he followed the career pattern of his mentor, E.P. Thompson. In another recent case, Michael Ignatieff has become a "moral philosopher" as well as television personality, in Britain, commenting through the media on the current crisis of direction in the Western world. Both these relatively young historians earned solid reputations as researchers and writers in British history prior to these full or partial career moves. Commitment is obviously the overriding factor in these cases.

Inevitably the question of the pressures of professionalism recurs. It seems characteristic of the discipline that increasing demands have been made not only for more research, but also that prudent detachment be exercised in relation to the subject being studied. The historian as insulated judge, objective in his use of accumulated facts (regardless of whether the historian can or should be detached from his subject) seems to be the preferred image. Yet the historian is part of his own times; indeed, his very motivation in becoming a historian undoubtedly relates to some latent, immediate interest in his own upbringing. It might be argued that detachment has drawbacks, as does total commitment. It is in the intersection of present concerns with historical precedents that we come to know ourselves. Jean Elder, an historian at the University of British Columbia, has made such a point in arguing for the relevance of that old standby, English constitutional history, in discussing the current state of the Canadian constitution.[14] Indeed, in its heyday the study of English constitutional history, at Oxford at least, was considered to be a way of teaching the deeper significance of history—as the unfolding of national progress—to undergraduates. Most honours history students, certainly before the First World War, became members of the governing class rather than scholars, a fact their tutors at Oxford were very conscious of. Constitutional history was considered to be a means of inspiration and motivation for these future leaders rather than a training ground for future scholars.

Research in British history continues outside Canada's formal university departments. An increasing number of works of high quality are being produced by historians not employed in regular university departments (M. Labarge, P. Munche, M. Distad, P. Malcolmson, M. Johnson, R. Stewart). Similarly eminent Canadian historians of Great Britain such as Martin Havran and Peter Marsh can still be found in departments outside Canada in the expatriate tradition. Thus the Canadian contribution to the field is not confined to history departments in this country.

British history itself may from time to time lose a good scholar or dip in enrolment, but its role continues to be significant. As John Norris, who now teaches the history of medicine, put it, Canada is in danger of becoming a "parish pump nation" through excessive parochialism.[15] Arthur Lower, himself a strong Canadian nationalist, once stated concerning British history: "We should not worry about imitativeness or anything of that sort. We should be ready to understand and accept and be proud of our heritage, which is an English heritage."[16] All may not agree with the notion of pride expressed by Lower, but there can be little doubt that the study of Britain's past is in a very real sense another way of knowing ourselves.[17]

Notes

NOTE ON SOURCES

Much of my research time was spent in university archives across Canada and in one case outside (Columbia for the Brebner Papers). Second only to this archival activity has been the considerable number of interviews conducted. I am deeply grateful to many people who made this book possible, through advice on sources as well as time spent on personal reflections and permissions to use various materials. Rather than identify particular persons, I prefer to thank everyone collectively. In some cases it was not possible to interview certain individuals or to mention their important contributions. This omission is more a matter of schedule rather than any question of a scale of importance attached to interviews and the like. Themes often dictated the direction of my writing and it was not possible to integrate every area of historical activity.

A book of this nature would not be possible without ground-breaking work by Canadian historians. In many places this book of necessity has been one of synthesis and a great many books, articles, unpublished papers, and theses have been of enormous help.

CHAPTER ONE: CANADIANS AND THEIR HISTORY

1 Fred Schneider, "The Habit of Deference: The Imperial Factor and the 'University Question' in Upper Canada," *Journal of British Studies* XVII, 1 (1977).
2 Arthur Lower interview, Kingston, Ontario, 29 July 1985.
3 *Report of Text Book Commission, 1907,* by order of the Province of Ontario (Toronto 1907), Appendix III: History of School Text Books, 20–9.
4 There are fine collections of old textbooks at various provincial archives as well as other locations such as the Ontario Institute for Studies in Education (OISE) in Toronto.
5 Frank Underhill interview conducted by W.D. Meickle, 10 September 1968, 15, vol. 95, Underhill Papers (Public Archives of Canada).
6 James T. Shotwell "Some Reminiscences," John Bartlett Brebner Papers (Rare Books and Manuscript Library, Columbia University), 5–6.
7 Ibid., 5.
8 W.J. Robertson, *Public School History of England and Canada* (Toronto 1897), 106.
9 Ibid., 19.
10 Spencer A. Jones to Chief Superintendent, 21 November 1866, Ministry of Education Records (RG2), Series C-5, Textbook Correspondence and Memoranda 1865–76 (Archives of Ontario).

11 Mary Leslie to Minister of Education, 15 October 1906, Education Department Text
    Book Records, D-9-A, Box 8 (Archives of Ontario).
12 Arthur Lower interview.
13 Report of debate, *Globe*, 2 December 1893.
14 *Globe*, 19 April 1894.
15 *Empire*, 4 December 1093.
16 See Charles W. Humphries, "The Banning of a Book in British Columbia," *BC
    Studies* no. 1 (1968–9), 1–12.
17 Mack Eastman, "Speech to Ladies of the Local Council," 5 February 1923, S. Mack
    Eastman Papers (University of British Columbia Archives).
18 Goldwin Smith to G.W. Ross, 7 June 1895, Ministry of Education Records, Series
    D-7, Box 11 (Archives of Ontario).
19 *Globe*, 27 November 1893.
20 Kenneth Bell, "History Teaching in Schools," *University Monthly* x, 7 (1910), 383.
21 Walter N. Sage, "Preliminary Report on the Teaching of History in the Elementary
    Schools of Canada," W.N. Sage Papers, pp 15, 21, 25, 43 (University of British
    Columbia Archives).
22 See George S. Tomkins, *A Common Countenance: Stability and Change in the
    Canadian Curriculum* (Scarborough, Ont. 1986), 226.
23 George Brown, *Building the Canadian Nation* (Toronto, 1942), 442.
24 *A Study of National History Textbooks in the Schools of Canada and the United States,*
    American Council on Education, Publication No. 2 (Washington, DC 1947), 56–7.
25 Carl Berger, *The Writing of Canadian History: Aspects of English-Canadian
    Historical Writing since 1900*, 2nd ed. (Toronto 1986), 35.
26 E.E. Rose interview, Toronto, 26 July 1985.

CHAPTER TWO: BIRTH OF A DISCIPLINE

1 A good background for these considerations can be furnished by A. Dwight Culler,
   The Victorian Mirror of History (New Haven, CT 1985) and Rosemary Jann, *The Art
   and Science of Victorian History* (Columbus, OH 1985).
2 T.W. Heyck, *The Transformation of Intellectual Life in Victorian England* (London
   1982).
3 Philippa Levine, *The Amateur and the Professional: Antiquarians, Historians and
   Archaeologists in Victorian England, 1838–1886* (Cambridge 1986), 157.
4 Reba Sofer, "Nation, Duty, Character and Confidence: History at Oxford,
   1850–1914," *Historical Journal* 30, 1 (1987), 77–104.
5 Heyck, *Transformation of Intellectual Life*, 172.
6 Henry Hallam (1777–1859), lawyer and author of books on constitutional history
   and the Middle Ages, was one of the first English historians to make extensive use of
   documents. Vaughan was professor of history at the University College, London,
   from 1834 to 1843.
7 Sir Daniel Wilson, Journal, 9 March 1891, D. Wilson Papers, B65-0014 (University
   of Toronto Archives).
8 Ian M. Drummond, *Political Economy at the University of Toronto: A History of the*

Department, 1888–1982 (Toronto 1983), 22.

9 See Alon Kadis, *The Oxford Economists in the Late Nineteenth Century* (Oxford 1982).

10 Drummond, *Political Economy at the University of Toronto*, 9.

11 Carl Berger, *The Writing of Canadian History: Aspects of English-Canadian Historical Writing since 1900*, 2nd ed. (Toronto 1986), 24. See also Bernard Semmel, *Imperialism and Social Reform* (Garden City, NY 1960), Ch. 11.

12 Berger, *Writing of Canadian History*, 6.

13 Richard T. Ely exchanged many letters with Ashley. They are found chiefly in the Ely Papers, held at the Wisconsin State Historical Society Archives in Madison.

14 W.J. Ashley to G.W. Ross, Minister of Education Records, 17 July 1892, Series D-7, Box 11 (Archives of Ontario).

15 Halford Vaughan was Regius Professor from 1848 to 1858. Vaughan was a great speaker and had a wide range of friends but few writings. Smith, however, was succeeded by the infinitely more important William Stubbs.

16 Letter to *Daily News*, 20 November 1861. The most complete treatment of Smith's life is Elizabeth Wallace, *Goldwin Smith: Victorian Liberal* (Toronto 1957).

17 Goldwin Smith, *Lectures on the Study of History: Delivered in Oxford, 1859–61* (Toronto 1873), Lecture II, 79.

18 Ibid., 90.

19 Goldwin Smith, *A Trip to England* (Toronto 1888), 54.

20 Ibid., 1–2.

21 Goldwin Smith to George Wrong, 2 August 1900, George M. Wrong Papers (Thomas Fisher Rare Book Library, University of Toronto).

22 Lecture II, 160.

CHAPTER THREE: THE RISING PROFESSION

1 W.D. Meikle, "And Gladly Teach: G.M. Wrong and the Department of History at the University of Toronto" (PH.D. thesis, Michigan State University 1977), 20–4.

2 A.F. Bowker, "Truly Useful Men: Maurice Hutton, George Wrong, James Mavor and the University of Toronto, 1880–1927" (PH.D. thesis, University of Toronto 1975), 75.

3 G.M. Wrong, *Historical Study in the University and the Place of Mediaeval History* (Toronto 1895), 19.

4 Ibid., 18.

5 Ibid., 5.

6 Daniel Wilson to G.W. Ross, 19 October 1891, Ministry of Education Records, Series D-7, Box 14 (Archives of Ontario).

7 *Varsity*, 7 November 1894.

8 These events have even become the subject matter of a play—*The Dismissal* (Erin, Ont., 1978) by James Reaney.

9 *Report of the Commissioners on the Discipline and Other Matters in the University of Toronto* (Toronto 1895), Exhibit E, 29 (copy in University of Toronto Archives).

10 Meikle, "And Gladly Teach," 47.

11 Ashley to Wrong, 8 May 1905, Wrong Papers.
12 Ralph Hodder-Williams, "The Tutorial Experiment," *U of T Monthly* xv (1915), 203.
13 A.B. McKillop, "The Research Ideal and the University of Toronto, 1870–1906," *Transactions of the Royal Society of Canada*, series IV, XX (1982), 253–84.
14 Michael Perceval-Maxwell, "The History of History at McGill," unpublished paper, 2 April 1981, James McGill Society, 11–12.
15 See Charles W. Colby, "The Craftsmanship of the Historian," in *The Writing of History* (New York 1926), 87.
16 Carl Berger, *The Writing of Canadian History: Aspects of English-Canadian Historical Writing since 1900*, 2nd ed. (Toronto 1986), 17.
17 Basil Williams to Principal, Report on History Department of McGill University, 31 December 1921, 1, Sir Arthur Currie Papers (McGill University Archives).
18 Waugh to Currie, 13 August 1925, Currie Papers.
19 Maxwell Cohen, "He Startled the Prairies," *McGill News* XXX, 2 (1948), 10.
20 Ibid.
21 H.N. Fieldhouse, Department of History, 1933–4, 34, *President's Reports* (University of Manitoba Archives).
22 Ibid.
23 "Notes on Study of Colonial Policy, 1923," Walter Sage Papers, Box X (University of British Columbia Archives).
24 "Lectures on English Constitutional History by C.B. Edwards, B.A., Lecturer, 1905–1906," 55, Landon Personal Papers (University of Western Ontario Archives).
25 Ibid., 64.
26 Richard V. Bannon to H.P. McPherson, 10 July 1935, Bannon Papers (St. Francis Xavier University Archives).
27 J.W. Falconer to Sir Joseph Flavelle, 10 September 1911, Case 38, file 1910–25, Flavelle Papers (Queen's University Archives). Also quoted in Michael Bliss, *A Canadian Millionaire* (Toronto 1978), 203.
28 Memoir of Sir Ray Wilson (personal memorials in possession of Hugh McDougall, Vice Principal, St. Michael's College School, Toronto).
29 Memoir of Agnes Wyatt McDougall, personal memorials.
30 C.P. Stacey, *A Date with History* (Ottawa 1986), 15.
31 G.W. Wrong to Frank Underhill, 14 March 1912, Underhill Papers.
32 Underhill interview, conducted by Meickle, "And Gladly Teach," 11.
33 Ibid.
34 "Introduction" notes and quotations, personal memorabilia (Mount St. Bernard College, Antigonish, Nova Scotia).

CHAPTER FOUR: NATION, WARS AND EMPIRE

1 See Carl Berger, *The Sense of Power: Studies in the Ideas of Canadian Imperialism, 1867–1914* (Toronto 1970).
2 See *Dictionary of National Biography* entry as well as Semmel, *Imperialism and*

Social Reform, 199.

3 Alon Kadish, *The Oxford Economists in the Late Nineteenth Century* (Oxford 1982), 49.

4 Goldwin Smith to James Bryce, 11 January 1902, Smith Papers, reel 12 (microfilm copy; original in Cornell University Archives).

5 See Ramsay Cook, *The Regenerators: Social Criticism in Late Victorian English Canada* (Toronto 1985), 154.

6 Dr. A.M. Thompson to the Rev. L.J. McPherson, 23 March 1900, Lauchlin J. McPherson Papers (St. Francis Xavier University Archives).

7 See John Kendle, *The Round Table Movement and Imperial Union* (Toronto 1975).

8 Ralph Hodder-Williams to G.M. Wrong, 23 September 1915, Wrong papers.

9 J.W. Dafoe to G.M. Wrong, 16 October 1916, Wrong Papers.

10 Clarence Perkins to President E.E. Braithwaite, 28 June 1919. Dean of Arts Letters 1910–28, Box 20, Faculty Appointments (University of Western Ontario Archives).

11 See R. Douglas Francis, *Frank H. Underhill: Intellectual Provocateur* (Toronto 1986), 30. The Francis biography appeared after much of the work was completed on this book.

12 D.G. Creighton, "The Ogdensburg Agreement and F.H. Underhill," in *The Passionate Observer* (Toronto 1980), 122.

13 Francis, *Underhill*, 79–80. More should be learned in the biography of Falconer by James G. Greenlee (Toronto 1987).

14 Lower interview.

15 Berger, *The Writing of Canadian History*, 134.

16 Lower interview.

17 H.N. Fieldhouse to President S.E. Smith, n.d., c. October 1940, Presidents' Papers (UA20), Box 27, fd. 13 (University of Manitoba Archives).

18 Cohen, "He Startled the Prairies," 44.

19 Fieldhouse to S.E. Smith, 20 May 1940, Presidents' Papers, Box 27, fd. 13.

20 "A Few Canadians" to President S.E. Smith, 30 September 1940, Presidents' Papers, Box 27, fd. 13.

21 Ibid., H.N. Fieldhouse to S.E. Smith, 18 July 1940.

22 Ibid.

23 Ibid.

24 B. Wilkinson, "Hitler's New Order," *University of Toronto Quarterly* XI, 1 (1941).

25 B. Wilkinson, "Canada's Place in an English-Speaking Union," *Saturday Night*, 30 November 1940.

26 Sydney Hermant interview, Toronto, 9 June 1987.

27 B. Wilkinson, "Introduction to Stories from Canadian History," 17 September 1944. Scripts were published by the Imperial Optical Company. Copies can be found in the University of Toronto Archives.

28 R.M. Saunders, "Oliver Cromwell," 28 January 1945.

29 George W. Brown, "Confidential Memorandum at the Bowmanville Officers' Internment Camp, 1942–44," Brown Papers (University of Toronto Archives).

30 Dale R. Brown, "Confidential Report of Educational Work in Prisoner-of-War

Camps in Canada, January 1–March 31, 1944," in Reports, 1940–5, Herman Boeschenstein Papers (University of Toronto Archives).

31 D.J. McDougall, "Report of a Lecture Given to Prisoners of War at Gravenhurst, December 9, 1944," 2. McDougall Papers (University of Toronto Archives).

32 D.J. McDougall, "Report on Lectures Given at the Prisoners of War Camp in Bowmanville During the Winter of 1943–44," 4, McDougall Papers (University of Toronto Archives).

33 Ibid., 8.

34 W.E.C. Harrison, *The Universities Are Dangerous* (Toronto 1941), 27.

35 Ibid., 1.

CHAPTER FIVE: THE VIEW FROM MORNINGSIDE HEIGHTS

1 J.B. Brebner, "Keystone in the Arch?", *Varsity Graduate* (January 1957).

2 J.B. Brebner to J.M.S. Careless, 21 April 1954. Correspondence, John Bartlet Brebner Papers (Rare Books and Manuscript Library, Columbia University).

3 Subject File, Records of the Department of History (University of Toronto Archives).

4 J.B. Brebner to Archibald MacMechan, 2 January 1926, MacMechan Papers, Dalhousie University Archives, quoted in George Rawlyk "J.B. Brebner and the Writing of Canadian History," *Journal of Canadian Studies* XIII (1978), 87.

5 J.B. Brebner to Sir Robert Falconer, 12 February 1929, Brebner Papers.

6 J.B. Brebner to J.M.S. Careless, 21 April 1954, Brebner Papers.

7 R.K. Webb interview, New York City, 21 December 1985.

8 Comments on time analysis sheet 1933–4, 2, Advisory Committee on Educational Policy, Columbia University, Brebner Papers.

9 J.T. Shotwell, "Some Reminiscences," 9.

10 Ibid., 11.

11 J.B. Brebner, "Oxford, Toronto and Columbia," *Columbia University Quarterly* XXIII (1931), 231.

12 Ibid., 227.

13 D.G. Creighton, "John Bartlet Brebner: A Man of His Times," in *The Passionate Observer* (Toronto 1980), 168.

14 Brebner, "Oxford, Toronto and Columbia," 225.

15 J.B. Brebner to J.M.S. Careless, 21 April 1954, Brebner Papers.

16 Ibid. The essay was published in *Essays in Canadian History, presented to George MacKinnon Wrong for his 80th Birthday* (Toronto 1939).

17 Ibid.

18 J.B. Brebner to J.W. Dafoe, 14 October 1938, Correspondence, Brebner Papers.

19 J.B. Brebner to F. Clarke, 14 October 1940, Correspondence, Brebner Papers.

20 J.B. Brebner to Harold Innis, 10 January 1940, Harold Innis Papers (University of Toronto Archives).

21 J.B. Brebner to Cyril James, 2 April 1941, Correspondence, Brebner Papers.

22 Stuart Ayers to J.B. Brebner, 13 August 1942, Correspondence, Brebner Papers.

23 J.B. Brebner to Harold Innis, 19 January 1943, Innis Papers.

24 Newsclip, New York Herald Tribune Bureau, London, 3 November 1942, File

"Britain," J.B. Brebner Papers.
25 J.B. Brebner to S. Piercy, 19 February 1944, Correspondence, Brebner Papers.
26 W.W. Norton to J.B. Brebner, 2 December 1942, Correspondence, Brebner Papers.
27 J.B. Brebner and Allan Nevins, *The Making of Modern Britain: A Short Story* (New York 1943), 11.
28 Dr. Ernest Barker, "Family Portraits," *Observer*, 28 November 1943.
29 T.J. Somers to J.B. Brebner, 22 July 1944, Correspondence, Brebner Papers.
30 J.B. Brebner to W.W. Norton, 19 July 1943, Correspondence, Brebner Papers.
31 W.W. Norton to J.B. Brebner, 21 April 1944, Correspondence, Brebner Papers.
32 J.B. Brebner to J.M.S. Careless, 21 April 1954, Brebner Papers.
33 E. Larkin letter to author, 29 October 1985.
34 J.B. Stewart interview, Antigonish, Nova Scotia, 17 May 1985.
35 E. Larkin to author, 29 October 1985.
36 Bernard Semmel interview, New York City, 21 December 1985.
37 E. Larkin to author, 29 October 1985.
38 W.S. MacNutt, introduction to J.B. Brebner, *The Neutral Yankees of Nova Scotia* (Carleton Library ed. 1969) xvii.
39 Webb interview.
40 J.B. Brebner to Madame Halévy, 19 March 1948, Correspondence, Brebner Papers.
41 Semmel interview.
42 Graham interview, Charlottetown, 12 October 1985.
43 J.B. Brebner, "The Contracting British Empire," *Alumni News*, May 1948.
44 J.B. Brebner, "The Democratic Functions of Government," 6, Brebner Papers.
45 Ibid.
46 J.B. Brebner, "History and the World of Today: The Problem of Synthesis," Address at Dinner of Society of Older Graduates of Columbia on 16 April 1947, 3, Brebner Papers.
47 J.B. Brebner to J. Edgar Hoover, 14 December 1949, Correspondence, Brebner Papers.
48 Harry Crowe to J.B. Brebner, 11 May 1950, Correspondence, Brebner Papers.
49 Letter to New York *Daily News*, 10 October 1952.
50 11 December 1943.
51 Vol. I (1949), 8.
52 Convocation oration given at Cathedral of St. John the Divine, 31 October 1954. Printed text supplied by Dr. Olive Brose.
53 Letter from D.C. Masters to author, 5 December 1985.
54 Rawlyk, "J.B. Brebner and the Writing of Canadian History," 87.
55 Printed texts of reports are found in the Brebner Papers.
56 "New Brunswick and Nova Scotia, February, 1944," 1–2, Brebner Papers.
57 Ibid.
58 Ibid., 4.
59 Ibid., 8.
60 Ibid., 8–9.
61 Ibid., 10.

62 Ibid.
63 Ibid., 10, 11
64 R.C. Lodge, Comments on J.B. Brebner *Scholarship for Canada*, 2, Brebner Papers.
65 J.B. Brebner to Editor of *The Star*, 21 December 1950, Correspondence, Brebner Papers.
66 J.B. Brebner to President Falconer, 12 February 1929, Correspondence, Brebner Papers.
67 J.B. Brebner to E.K. Brown, 16 February 1945, Correspondence, Brebner Papers.
68 J.B. Brebner, "History and the World of Today," 1.
69 R.K. Webb interview.
70 Carl Berger, *The Writing of Canadian History: Aspects of English-Canadian Historical Writing since 1900*, 2nd ed. (Toronto 1986), 159.

CHAPTER SIX: AN INTERVIEW WITH GERALD S. GRAHAM

1 William Lawson Grant (1872–1935), educated at Queen's University and Oxford. He was Beit Lecturer in colonial history at Oxford, Professor of Colonial History at Queen's, and finally Headmaster of Upper Canada College, 1917–35.
2 George W. Trevelyan, Harold Temperley, Ernest Barker, G.P. Gooch, and Dame Lillian Penson were all well-known British historians of the interwar period.
3 Gerhard Ritter (1888–1967), German historian.
4 Robert Spencer, retired professor of German history, University of Toronto.
5 William L. Langer and Frederick Merk, Harvard historians. Roger B. Merriman (1876–1945) was Gurney Professor of History and Political Science after 1929 and Master of Eliot House, Harvard.
6 George Glazebrook was a member of the University of Toronto Department of History at various times, as well as a federal civil servant both during and after the Second World War. He was ambassador to the United States from 1953 to 1956.
7 Canadian-born A.L. Burt was Professor of British History at Minnesota, where he also supervised many theses in Canadian history. R.H. Tawney (1880–1962) was a famous British economic historian and Christian socialist.

CHAPTER SEVEN: THE GENERATIONS SINCE 1945

1 Maurice Careless interview conducted by P. Abators, 13 July 1983, B83-0038 (University of Toronto Archives).
2 Maurice Careless interview, Antigonish, NS, 19 October 1985.
3 David Spring interview, Toronto, 24 July 1985.
4 John Norris interview, Vancouver, 26 May 1986.
5 J.B. Conacher interview, Kingston, 12 July 1985.
6 E.R. Adair, "The Canadian Contribution to Historical Science," *Culture* IV (1943), 65.
7 Michael Powicke interview, Toronto, 17 June 1986.
8 Zvi Razi, "Family, Land and the Village Community in Late Medieval England," *Past and Present* 93 (1981), 4–36.

9 Hugh MacCallum, "A.S.P. Woodhouse: Teacher and Scholar," *University of Toronto Quarterly* LIV, 1 (1984), 7.
10 David Spring interview.
11 John Beattie interview, Toronto, 26 July 1985.
12 C.B. Macpherson interview, Toronto, 16 July 1985.
13 Vincent Bladen interview, conducted by C.R. Myers, 4 January 1974, B74-0038 (University of Toronto Archives).
14 Hilda Neatby to Vincent Massey, 14 January 1956, Vincent Massey Papers (by permission of the Master and Senior Fellows, Massey College, University of Toronto, and Professor B. Neatby).
15 Berger, *The Writing of Canadian History: Aspects of English-Canadian Historical Writing since 1900*, (Toronto 1986), 180.
16 J.M.S. Careless, preface in *The Gladstonian Turn of Mind: Essays Presented to J.B. Conacher* (Toronto 1985), ed. by Bruce Kinzer, xiii.
17 A.P. Thornton interview, Toronto, 17 July 1985.
18 Patrick McGrath, obituary, Annual Report of University Council to Court, Bristol 1970–1, 4–7 and W.L. Morton, obituary, *Canadian Historical Review* LII, 3 (1971), 355–6.
19 Stanford Reid interview, Guelph, 25 July 1985.
20 Dean H.N. Fieldhouse, "Appendix on History," in "Revised and Continued Interim Report of the General Committee of the Humanities Group," 10 June 1949, Dean Fieldhouse Files (McGill University Archives), 22.
21 Letter from Goldwin Smith to author, 13 June 1985.
22 Careless interview, Antigonish.
23 E.E. Rose interview, Toronto, 26 July 1985.

CHAPTER EIGHT: CONTEMPORARY TEACHING AND RESEARCH

1 J.B. Conacher, "Graduate Studies in History in Canada: The Growth of Doctoral Programmes," *Historical Papers* (1975), 3.
2 Albert Tucker interview, Toronto, 6 August 1985.
3 David Cannadine, "British History: Past, Present—and Future?" *Past and Present*, 116 (1987), 169–91.
4 Ibid., 175.
5 Ibid., 173.
6 Harry Granter interview, Halifax, 13 June 1985.
7 J.M. Robson interview, Toronto, 16 June 1987.
8 John Matthews interview, Kingston, 5 June 1986. I interviewed Melvin Wiebe at Kingston, 11 July 1985, and Donald Schurman also at Kingston, 12 July 1985.
9 Interviews in Hamilton, 22 July 1985, with Richard Rempel, McMaster Vice-President Leslie King, and John Passmore.
10 James McConica interview, Toronto, 12 July 1986.
11 John Beattie interview.
12 E.E. Rose interview.
13 Robert Malcolmson interview, 5 June 1986.

14 Jean Elder, "Stubbs's Constitutional History: A Shelved Document," *Queen's Quarterly* LXXXVIII, 3 (1981), 515–22.
15 John Norris interview.
16 Arthur Lower interview.

INDEX